Introducing Electronic Text Analysis

'This is an interesting and exceptionally accessible book, which will especially be of use to readers who are new to corpus-based analysis. Svenja Adolphs covers a wide range of corpus techniques and concepts (keywords, concordances, frequency data, collocation, semantic prosodies) without overwhelming the reader with too much information. There are numerous chances to follow up on topics with suggested further reading, while the use of study questions and the website linked to the book are also useful aids. I will be recommending it to my students.'
Paul Baker, Lancaster University

Introducing Electronic Text Analysis presents the study of text and discourse carried out with the use of computers. It offers a practical guide to ways in which the use of computers can complement more traditional types of text and discourse analysis along with a range of sample analyses of contemporary English language in use.

The book discusses the underlying principles and concepts relevant to electronic text analysis, many of which are used in the area of corpus linguistics with the aim of enhancing language descriptions. It also provides an overview of different types of electronic text collections including both spoken and written English.

Introducing a number of key analytical techniques, such as the study of concordance data and frequency information, Svenja Adolphs then looks at a range of applied contexts in which electronic text analysis plays an increasingly prominent role. These include the exploration of literary texts, the study of ideology in text and discourse, and the use of electronic text analysis in the English Language Teaching context, all of which are complemented with a discussion of further fields of application in the final chapter.

With abundant illustrative examples and a glossary of definitions of main concepts, this book provides an accessible and thorough description of the underlying principles of electronic text analysis and is supported by a companion website with links to on-line corpora so that students can apply their knowledge to further study.

Svenja Adolphs is Lecturer in Applied Linguistics at the University of Nottingham.

Introducing Electronic Text Analysis

A practical guide for language and literary studies

Svenja Adolphs

Routledge
Taylor & Francis Group

LONDON AND NEW YORK

First published 2006
by Routledge
2 Park Square, Milton Park, Abingdon, Oxon OX14 4RN

Simultaneously published in the USA and Canada
by Routledge
270 Madison Ave, New York, NY 10016

Routledge is an imprint of the Taylor & Francis Group, an informa business

Typeset in Perpetua by Keyword Group Ltd.
Printed and bound in Great Britain by The Cromwell Press,
Trowbridge, Wiltshire

British Library Cataloguing in Publication Data
A catalogue record for this book is available from the British Library

Library of Congress Cataloging-in-Publication Data

Adolphs, Svenja.
    Introducing electronic text analysis / by Svenja Adolphs.
        p. cm.
    Includes bibliographical references.
    ISBN 0-415-32021-6 (pbk.)
    1. Discourse analysis–Data processing. I. Title.
    P302.3.A36 2006
    401'.410285–dc22

                                    2005037451

ISBN10: 0-415-32022-4 (hbk)
ISBN10: 0-415-32021-6 (pbk)
ISBN10: 0-203-08770-4 (ebk)

ISBN13: 978-0-415-32022-1 (hbk)
ISBN13: 978-0-415-32021-4 (pbk)
ISBN13: 978-0-203-08770-1 (ebk)

Contents

**4   Exploring words and phrases in use:
basic techniques**   **51**

5   The electronic analysis of literary texts   **64**

6   Electronic text analysis, language and ideology   **80**

List of tables and illustrations

Tables

Illustrations

Preface

There are a number of competing priorities when it comes to writing introductions, and this one is no exception. Decisions had to be made as to whether to focus more on theoretical or practical questions, on breadth or detail, on technical or applied issues. With an introduction to electronic text analysis these decisions are made even more difficult as the field is moving forward at an incredible pace, reflecting the speed at which technology advances in this day and age. And sometimes it can seem as though the rapid development of technology exceeds the development of theories and models that are needed in order to make sense of the kind of evidence that we are now able to generate from texts and through texts.

The ease of access to electronic texts and to analysis software means that electronic text analysis is increasingly being utilised by researchers in a range of diverse areas in the arts and humanities and in the social sciences. A core aim in writing this book has been to make the techniques developed in the area of corpus linguistics more accessible to non-corpus specialists. This has also informed the choice of title of this publication. Electronic Text Analysis is used as a broad term that includes the analysis of single texts as well as text collections. It also has a slightly different focus to the core business of corpus linguistics in that its main motivation is not always that of extracting patterns with a view to develop language descriptions.

There is, however, a strong influence of corpus linguistics in this field, and much of the content of the book will be familiar territory for corpus linguists. In order to make the book accessible to non-corpus specialists, I have tried to strike a balance between the discussion of theoretical issues and the illustration of different types of analyses with examples from electronic texts and text collections. Where possible emphasis has been placed on the discussion of possible applications in different areas, as well as on the resources that are required to start work in electronic text analysis.

In terms of the types of texts that form the basis of the majority of the sample analyses and discussions in this book, the focus is on contemporary spoken and written English that, for the most part, has not been generated for the purpose of electronic communication. As such the book does not elaborate on the electronic analysis of texts from a diachronic perspective, nor on the analysis of electronic genres such as e-mail, Internet Relay Chat or text messaging discourse for example. However, the methods and approaches discussed in this publication may be applied to such genres where they would contribute to systematic explorations of vocabulary, context and style.

Acknowledgements

While writing this book I have been very fortunate to be able to draw on the support and encouragement of colleagues, friends and family.

I would like to thank Ronald Carter for his continuous support of this book and other projects, for patiently reading and commenting on various drafts, for allowing me to draw on articles we have co-written, and for simply being the best mentor one could ever wish for.

I am also grateful to the many people who have generously provided me with comments, information and points of discussion related to various parts of this publication, and I have particularly benefited from the friendly support from my colleagues here at Nottingham.

Special thanks to Sarah Atkins who has been a great help in the final stages of preparation of the manuscript, and to Dawn Knight for her help with a number of corpus searches and formatting issues. Thanks also to Paul Baker, Cornelius Grebe, Norbert Schmitt and Peter Stockwell for providing detailed comments on drafts of this book, or parts of it.

I am particularly grateful to Louisa Semlyen, Elizabeth Johnston and Kate Ahl at Routledge for their guidance, help and encouragement with this publication.

Parts of this book draw on articles that have previously been published and thanks go to the following sources and co-authors for allowing me to use this material for the purpose of this publication:

To the publishers of *Poetica* for: 'Corpus stylistics: point of view and semantic prosodies in To The Lighthouse' (2002) 58: 7–20 (with Ronald Carter); to the University of Murcia for: 'The Meaning of Genetics' (2003) 57–76 (with Craig Hamilton and Brigitte Nerlich) and for 'And she's like 'it's terrible like'': Spoken Discourse, Grammar and Corpus Analysis' (2003) 45–56 (with Ronald Carter), in *International Journal of English Studies*.

Many of the corpus examples in this book are taken from the Cambridge and Nottingham Corpus of Discourse in English (CANCODE), and I am grateful to Cambridge University Press for allowing me to use extracts and concordance data from the CANCODE corpus. CANCODE is a 5-million-word computerized corpus of spoken English, made up of recordings from a variety of settings in the countries of the UK and Ireland. CANCODE was built by Cambridge University Press and the University of Nottingham and it forms part of the Cambridge International Corpus (CIC). Sole copyright of the corpus resides with Cambridge University Press, from whom all permissions to reproduce material must be obtained.

Other corpora and archives that have been used in this book include the Bank of English ™, the Oxford Text Archive and the British National Corpus.

I am grateful to Collins Dictionaries for permission to use data from the Bank of English ™ and to the Oxford Text Archive for permission to use the concordance data from *Anna Karenina* in chapter five. Data cited from the British National Corpus has been extracted from the British National Corpus Online service and from the British National Corpus, managed and distributed respectively by Oxford University Computing Services on behalf of the BNC Consortium. All rights in the texts cited are reserved.

Svenja Adolphs
Nottingham, December 2005

1 Introduction

The field of electronic text analysis has been expanding rapidly over the past decades. This is partly due to advances in information technology and software development, but also as a result of the growing interest in using electronic resources to complement more traditional approaches to the analysis of language and literature. The improved accessibility of computers has added to the increasing popularity of electronic text analysis, especially in the higher education context. The development of principled collections of electronic texts, also called corpora, has allowed a systematic exploration of recurring patterns in language in use, and this has become one of the main areas of enquiry in the emerging field referred to as corpus linguistics.

With courses and modules in corpus linguistics and computer-aided language analysis currently being offered in many university departments across the country, there is also a growing emphasis on integrating electronic tools and resources in analyses of literary works. At the same time, electronic text analysis is increasingly being utilised as a tool in a range of applied contexts, for example in the area of language teaching or the study of language and ideology. These areas of investigation make use of a range of methodologies that have originally been developed in the area of corpus linguistics with the aim of enhancing language description.

This book combines the description of a range of approaches and methodologies in this field with a discussion of a number of areas of language study in which electronic text analysis is being used, often by way of complementing more traditional, analytical approaches. The main aim throughout the book is to introduce key ideas and methodologies and to illustrate these, where appropriate, through attested examples of language data. The book is primarily intended for the non-expert user who wishes to draw on some of the methodologies developed in the field of corpus linguistics for the purpose of analysing electronic texts.

Electronic text analysis: corpus linguistics by another name?

There are a number of terms that describe traditions and methodologies of computer-aided language research. They include, amongst others, corpus linguistics,

Natural Language Processing (NLP) and Humanities Computing. The differences between these approaches lie in their overall research goals, the types of texts that they draw on, and the way in which the texts are analysed. While the methodologies described in this book are derived mainly from the corpus linguistic tradition, they are also applied to problems and texts that are not normally at the heart of this tradition. The term electronic text analysis has been adopted to reflect the different priorities in terms of data sources and research processes when we compare corpus linguistics as a tradition with other areas of computer-aided language research. As such, the term electronic text analysis has been chosen for its inclusive and broad meaning that relates to the analysis of any digitized text or text collection.

Research goals

To illustrate just some of the kinds of different orientations found in the diverse range of areas that use electronic text analysis, we will consider the examples of Natural Language Processing (NLP) and Humanities Computing in more detail. NLP is often geared towards developing models for particular applications, such as machine translation software for example. Sinclair (2004b) makes a useful distinction between *description* and *application* in this context. Language description here refers to the process of exploring corpus data with the aim of developing a better understanding of language in use, while an application refers to the deployment of language analysis tools with the aim of producing an output that has relevance outside of linguistics. Sinclair (2004b: 55) notes that the end users of language description are predominantly other linguists who are interested in empirical explorations of the way in which language is used. The end users of linguistic applications on the other hand are not necessarily linguists. They may be people who are simply users of the developed application, such as a spell checker or a machine translation system that has been developed on the basis of a textual resource. The research goal in this case is the successful development of an application rather than the comprehensive description of language in use. This distinction marks one of the differences in orientation between corpus linguistics and NLP.

Humanities Computing tends to be concerned with enhancing and documenting textual interpretations, often within a hermeneutic tradition. A number of specialist journals have emerged in this area, including *Computers and the Humanities*, and a substantial amount of research is devoted to making processes of textual interpretation more explicit to the research community by way of various types of documentation. Burnard (1999) highlights the need for this process:

> […] because the digital world so greatly increases access to original unmediated source material (or at least a simulation thereof), the esoteric techniques developed over the centuries in order to contextualise and thus comprehend

such materials will need to be made accessible to far more people. We urgently need to develop new methods of doing textual editing and textual exposition, appropriate to the coming digital textual deluge.

All of the fields above analyse electronic, i.e. digitised, text(s) and use, where appropriate, software tools to do so.

Textual resources

One of the main differences between the various traditions in electronic text analysis lie in the nature of the textual resources and in the way in which they have been assembled to become an object of study. A corpus tends to be defined as a collection of texts which has been put together for linguistic research with the aim of making statements about a particular language variety. Biber *et al*. (1998:4) point out in this context that a corpus-based approach 'utilises a large and principled collection of natural texts, known as a "corpus", as the basis for analysis'.

A single text might not be able to provide a balanced sample of any one language variety. The same applies to other texts that may exist in electronic format but have not been assembled to represent a principled sample of a language variety, such as an e-mail message, for example, or the world wide web. These can, of course, be assembled in a principled way and turned into a corpus for linguistic study. We will return to a discussion of the world wide web as a corpus in chapter two.

As far as the nature of the textual resource is concerned, there are core differences between naturally occurring discourse versus discourse that has been produced under experimental conditions, and between large-scale and small-scale texts and text collections. Since people who work in the discipline of corpus linguistics are often interested in the exploration of social phenomena, such as the relationship between patterns of usage and social context for example, naturally occurring discourse is required as the basis of any study. In order to be able to extract patterns from this type of discourse, the textual resources need to be substantial in size for the corpus linguist. This point takes us to the next issue.

Types of analysis

The way in which the corpus linguist approaches a text is through secondary analysis of concordance lines and frequency information (see Sinclair 2004a: 189). The close reading and interpretation of a single text is not the primary concern of the corpus linguist; instead the core research activity is the extraction of language patterns through the analysis of suitably sorted instances of particular lexical items and phrases (see Sinclair 2004a). This is not necessarily the approach taken by the particularly labour intensive and had to be carried out by a large number of people over a period of many years. There are a number of examples of manual concordance extraction since these initial bible studies, notably in relation to literary works such as Shakespeare collections, for example.

The first electronic text analysis tools were designed in the 1950s and initially only produced paper concordances. More interactive programs, which allowed for on-screen data manipulation, were developed in the 1960s and, with the increasing availability and access to personal computers since this time, concordance programs have been transferred from mainframe computers to PCs. As such, they became available to individual researchers in the early 1980s, which is also when the first multi-million word corpora were developed (see Kennedy 1998 for an overview). The interactive nature of current concordancing programs allows the researcher to manipulate the data in a number of different ways that facilitate the analysis of any emerging patterns.

Studying language: theory and practice

Descriptions of language and resulting theories can be based either on the observation of naturally occurring discourse in use or on the intuition of a person who uses a particular language. This key difference in the kind of data that forms the basis for language theory marks two different approaches: empiricism and rationalism. Put simply, rationalist approaches to language are concerned with the way in which the mind processes language, while empiricist approaches are based on the observation of naturally occurring data. As far as linguistic judgements are concerned, rationalism is associated with introspection, e.g. a native speaker making judgements about the meaning of a particular word based on intuition, while empiricism is associated with observing language in use, e.g. through a corpus of recorded discourse events.

The influential American linguist Noam Chomsky argued in the 1950s and 1960s that linguistic study should be concerned with the exploration of language competence, i.e. the internalized knowledge of a language, rather than language performance, the external use of a language (Chomsky 1965). The main argument behind this suggestion was that Chomsky regarded performance data as limited and limiting in terms of what it can reveal about our language competence. He argued that performance can be affected by external events and is thus not an adequate representation of a speaker-listener's language competence. At the same time, Chomsky noted that no collection of naturally occurring discourse can ever be substantial enough to be a true representation of a language (see McEnery and Wilson 2001: 5–12 for a discussion of these points).

These arguments had a considerable impact on the way in which linguistics developed in the time following the publication of Chomsky's ideas. However, with advances in technology and the development of machine-readable corpora, empiricist approaches to language study steadily regained popularity in the latter half of the twentieth century. This is partly because corpus studies have shown that native-speaker intuition can be unreliable when it comes to making judgements about language in use, and there are certain aspects of language that are simply not open to intuition, such as word frequency distributions for example. Furthermore, studies of naturally occurring data can be replicated and verified by other researchers which is not the case with those studies that are based entirely on the introspective judgements of one person.

However, native-speaker intuition does have a place in empirical language research. It informs the types of queries we address with the use of a corpus, as well as our analysis and interpretation of the language evidence a corpus can provide (see McEnery *et al.* 2006: 6–7). This chapter introduces a number of examples of empirical language studies that illustrate this interplay between intuition, language in use and its interpretation.

Why use electronic text analysis?

As outlined above, corpus linguistics is often discussed in terms of its stark contrast to Chomskyan linguistics, which focuses on language competence and favours native speaker intuition as the basis for linguistic theories. So, if we were to assume that native speaker intuition is an adequate basis on which to make statements about a language, then what are the advantages of using electronic text analysis of naturally occurring discourse? There are many ways in which electronic text analysis can facilitate language research and the remainder of this book aims to illustrate how this might be done in practice. However, before going into more detailed discussions, here is a brief summary of the key advantages of using electronic text analysis:

- The reliance on intuition in language research inevitably introduces a high degree of bias into the analysis/description. Using electronic text analysis to study naturally occurring discourse, on the other hand, is a more replicable process and any analysis can be verified by other researchers.
- In addition, electronic text analysis allows us to extract information about language that does not tend to be open to intuitive inspection. This includes information about word frequency and co-occurrence of particular words.
- Electronic text analysis allows us to manipulate language data in various ways to suit a particular research purpose. The use of software tools in this process leads to more accurate and consistent results in a very short amount of time.
- Once the data has been sorted in an accessible way, such as in a concordance output for example, we can carry out further analysis on the data. This analysis again helps to identify patterns that we might not be able to describe purely

on an intuitive basis. This includes the analysis of whether a word carries positive or negative connotations, and the semantic concepts that surround individual words. It also means that we can identify phrases and clusters of particular types of words.

- Electronic text analysis can be used at different stages in the analytical process, as required by the researcher. Frequency lists, for example, can give us a good initial overview of our data and further analyses can be carried out on the basis of the derived frequency information. At the same time, we can use electronic text analysis as a hypothesis testing device, where the starting point might be our intuition, which is followed by an analysis of a suitable corpus.

- Related to the last point is the division between qualitative and quantitative approaches and the direction of progression between the two. Electronic text analysis can be used in a quantitative way, such as through the use of frequency lists, and lead to a subsequent qualitative exploration. Or, it can be used as a secondary method that follows an initial qualitative exploration. An example of the latter approach would be an analysis of frequencies and distributions of a particular language function, such as the use of suggestions in spoken discourse, with the aim of collecting quantitative evidence for results that stem from initial qualitative analyses.

There are many more uses of electronic text analysis that will be discussed further in this volume. However, there are also instances where electronic text analysis might not be the right approach for a particular problem or research purpose. So far, electronic text analysis cannot easily handle representations that are not textual, such as images that form part of a text, particular graphological styles, or elements that are linked through hypertext (see Sinclair 2005). All of these components contribute to the meaning of a text but cannot currently be handled through electronic text analysis. Similarly, intonation and body language in spoken discourse cannot easily be analysed with methods of electronic text analysis, although various research projects are currently underway that explore the development of integrated searchable resources that includes textual, visual and audio elements.

Another factor that may limit the scope of electronic text analysis in any one study lies in the data resources that form the basis of the investigations. While the analysis of naturally occurring data can tell us a lot about language that we would otherwise not be able to describe, the results of our studies have to be assessed in relation to the data sets we use. If a particular word or phrase does not occur in a corpus, this is not necessarily an indication of its frequency in the language in general but tells us something about the data on which the frequency analysis was based. Any statements about the language of a particular textual resource thus have to be made with reference to the particular corpus or text which gives rise to them (see Hunston 2002: 22–3).

The scope of electronic text analysis

Access to computer resources and electronic texts has led to a considerable change in the way in which research in the arts and humanities and in the social sciences research has been conducted over the past two decades. The scope of electronic text analysis in this context is expanding with the development of new techniques to retrieve, analyse and represent electronic texts. It should be noted in this context that electronic text manipulation and analysis is not confined to the methods developed and used within the area of corpus linguistics. Other manipulations that are regularly applied to electronic text collections include for example the use of hypertext to enhance electronic versions of different types of text with added information ranging from translations to interpretative commentary. This type of resource enhancement has become a particularly popular approach for marking up literary texts where added information on authors and textual history, for example, can add to the usability of a text by a wide research community.

The types of methods that have traditionally been used by corpus linguists to facilitate research in lexicography have found their way into a range of areas, particularly those associated with the broader field of applied linguistics, as illustrated in the examples below:

- **English language teaching**. A large number of dictionaries now include descriptions of words and phrases that are based on corpus research. Other teaching materials, such as grammars and textbooks, are also benefiting more and more from the availability of evidence derived from a corpus (see for example Biber *et al.* 1999). A key advantage of using corpora in this context is that they can provide evidence on word frequencies and distributions in different discourse contexts, which constitutes important information for the language learner. Corpora can also be used as the basis for the description of phrases in a language, which again is of great benefit to the learner. And, finally, there is an increasing body of research that illustrates the discrepancies between the type of English we find in traditional teaching materials that are based on intuition, and the kind that we find in language corpora (see for example Gilmore 2004). As language descriptions evolve with the use of corpora, the integration of new insights into teaching materials seems to be an important next step. Chapter seven deals with these issues in more detail.
- **Language variation**. The use of large electronic text collections has facilitated the study of both synchronic and diachronic variation. While this book focuses mainly on contemporary English, the use of corpora plays an important and extensive part in the study of language development over time. In terms of diachronic variation, the continuous development of new corpora makes it possible to trace language changes over even very short periods of time, and the use of the internet as a resource for linguistic research can help

reveal some of the most recent developments in language use. The study of synchronic variation, on the other hand, takes a snapshot of a language at a particular point in time and explores patterns of use in different contexts (see for example Reppen *et al.* 2002). The latter has influenced a number of other areas including English language teaching, which benefits from context-sensitive descriptions of language use as they facilitate a more targeted approach.

- **Language and ideology**. Electronic text analysis has also found an application in the study of ideology (Stubbs 1996). Individual lexical items are being studied in a given corpus with reference to any patterns of usage that show some sort of bias or prejudice. The concept of 'semantic prosodies' developed by Louw (1993) has come to be instrumental in this context. The semantic prosody of a word is the 'shading' of the meaning of that word that can be uncovered through the systematic study of the word in use. The semantic prosody of an individual lexical item may not be immediately apparent through the use of intuition. The study of ideology in language is a particular concern of critical discourse analysts and the use of corpus linguistic methods has opened up a new way of collecting evidence to support theory and practice in this area. Orpin (2005) for example uses a corpus to study words that relate to 'corruption', and finds that words with a negative semantic prosody tend to be used to refer to activities outside of Britain while the same tendency does not apply to words that refer to activities inside Britain.

- **Forensic linguistics**. Forensic linguistics is concerned with the analysis of texts that are in any way relevant to the law. The particular texts that are studied span a wide range from police interviews to court proceedings (Cotterill 2001). In addition, any other documentation that has legal relevance falls under the remit of forensic linguistics. Electronic text analysis can be used to compare a specific document with a collection of texts where, for example, the aim is to uncover plagiarism or authorship. Forensic linguists sometimes combine corpus linguistic methods with statistics to assess the origin of documents that are relevant in a legal context (see Coulthard 1993).

- **Spoken discourse analysis**. Researchers in the area of spoken discourse analysis, while mainly concerned with detailed descriptions of lexical, grammatical and discoursal patterns in a given stretch of conversation, have more recently started to draw on multi-million word corpora for their studies (McCarthy 1998). Concordance searches and frequency counts, say for example of discourse markers, often act as a point of entry into the data, as these techniques can highlight particular patterns that can subsequently be subjected to a more qualitative analysis.

- **Sociolinguistics**. Sociolinguistics is concerned with the exploration of the relationship between social and linguistic variables. Electronic text analysis has been used to study the occurrence of gender-related language (Kjellmer

1986, Holmes 1994). More recently McEnery (2005) has carried out a large-scale corpus-based study of swearing in a number of different discourses. The social variables he considers in relation to bad language range from gender to social class to age, and illustrate the value of electronic text exploration in providing evidence as part of sociolinguistic research.

- **Corpus stylistics**. There has been a growing interest in the digitization of literary texts over the last decade. Such resources are often annotated with useful information about the particular text and presented as an integrated archive for the research community. Beyond the ease of access to archives of literary texts themselves and to metadata about the texts, there has been a growing interest in the exploration of literary texts through techniques that have been developed in the area of corpus linguistics (Semino and Short 2004). These techniques are applied to organize particular interpretative annotations that have been added to a given literary text or text collection, and can enhance the analysis of literary discourse either in its own right or as a complementary approach that is used alongside other techniques of interpretation. Chapter five will deal with such processes in more detail.
- **Comparing and analysing language varieties**. While the main focus of this book is on British English, the development of corpora of other, as well as of more specialized, varieties makes it possible to carry out analyses and comparisons of language use according to regional and national varieties. Recent corpus developments that focus on particular varieties include for example the *Scottish Corpus of Texts and Speech* (SCOTS), the *Limerick Corpus of Irish English* (LCIE), and the *International Corpus of English* (ICE).

Projects in electronic text analysis

Whether you are a student of language or literature, critical theory or history, or if you are studying for a degree in the social sciences, you will probably be working with electronic texts at some point. A project that uses software packages that allow you to manipulate and analyse your data might offer a new perspective on a particular problem. You may also be able to use electronic text analysis to complement more traditional types of analyses in your discipline and thus add another layer to your research.

There are a few things to keep in mind when embarking on a project that analyses digitized collections of texts.

Research questions

While the electronic analysis of texts allows us to address a variety of research questions, it is important to understand that there are certain limitations to using this approach in isolation. A collection of particular texts, or a corpus, is best suited to describe patterns of language use, but it is not well suited to describe single occurrences of lexical items or sequences, other than in the context of distributional analyses. Some lexical items or sequences may not at all occur in a given corpus, which highlights the fact that corpus research can only ever produce results that reflect the particular corpus that is being used for a study. Depending on the size and type of corpus that is being used, it may or may not be appropriate to suggest that results may be representative of general use of a language.

Another question to address at the outset is whether you are using corpus linguistic techniques simply to represent your existing data in a way that might facilitate your analysis and description of it, or whether you are trying to address a particular problem and therefore have to collect or identify data-sets that might be suitable to address the research question you have identified. There is a crucial difference between the two approaches. In the first case, corpus linguistic techniques are used to facilitate the analysis of a particular text or collection of texts, and are often used as a complementary approach. An example of this might be the analysis of a particular novel that you would like to explore in further detail by using corpus linguistic techniques. In the second case, corpus linguistic techniques are used to inform judgements about a particular language variety and may be the main approach in the analysis. An example of this approach would be a study of the language of media discourse. Such an approach means that a lot of thought has to be put into the question of corpus design to ensure that it reflects the language variety that is being studied. This issue will be addressed in more detail in chapter two.

Availability of texts

There are now a number of internet sites and archives which offer access to both spoken and written electronic texts, some of them free of charge. While it is possible to record and transcribe your own data or indeed to scan in written text to assemble a new corpus to your own specifications, these procedures can be time-consuming and may therefore be unsuitable for undergraduate assignments. Yet, this may be an option for more substantial pieces of assessment.

If you have a sufficient number of machine-readable texts that you would like to put together into a corpus you can use web-based corpus assemblers to make your data more manageable and easy to manipulate. If you are using texts that are not already part of an existing corpus, you need to give some thought to the issue of copyright. In some instances, although you may browse some electronic texts via the internet, copyright restrictions might mean that you are not allowed to store these texts in electronic format. Even the use of existing corpora may involve some sort of agreement between the publisher and the end-user that outlines the conditions under which the data may be used. It is advisable, where possible, to identify the copyright owner in the first instance and seek permission to use their data as part of your project.

Availability of software

If you are able to write your own programs to analyse your data then there are a number of publications and reference guides available that provide information on how to develop such programs for linguistic analysis.[3] However, if you do not have any programming background there are now a range of software packages available that will carry out the standard procedures of electronic text analysis for you. Some of these programs are available free of charge via the internet and others can be purchased and used off-line. Chapter two will deal with various software packages that are currently available in more detail.

Organization of the book

As might be predictable with a book on electronic text analysis, one of the core domains for resources and research in this area is the internet. Information about existing corpora and new corpus projects, access to text archives and software packages for electronic text analysis, corpus linguistics tutorials and other resources sites, tend to be available online.[4] This means that a book on electronic text analysis has to be complemented by a companion website which contains links to the key sites that are referred to in the book. This book is thus designed to be used in conjunction with the companion website, which will be regularly updated while the book is in print. Where reference is made to online resources, or where it would be beneficial to the reader to follow-up on further information that can be accessed via the internet, this has been indicated by italicizing the relevant terms in the text.

The book itself is structured in the following way. Following this general introduction, chapter two discusses a number of electronic text resources currently available and deals with issues such as design, size and representativeness of individual resources.

Chapter three introduces the analysis of frequencies as one of the key techniques used to gather information about individual texts and text resources. This type of quantitative approach will be discussed with reference to individual texts, as well as with reference to comparisons between texts and text collections.

Chapter four moves from a focus on the characterization of texts to the description of individual words and phrases in context. The use of concordance data as the basis for language description and interpretation will be discussed in more detail in this chapter.

Chapter five marks the transition from methodological issues in electronic text analysis to applied ones. This chapter deals with the analysis of literary texts, many of which are now readily available for use via the internet and CD-ROMs. The main focus is on the ways in which electronic text analysis can enhance and complement traditional stylistic analysis using both literary and non-literary corpora.

Chapter six deals with the analysis of ideology with the use of electronic text resources. Different methods will be explored to analyse the use of individual lexical items in different corpora with a view to uncovering traces of ideology in the particular discourse.

Corpus linguistics has had a considerable effect on the area of language teaching, notably because the study of authentic texts has revealed inconsistencies between the use of lexical items and grammatical structures in corpora and those found in traditional textbooks. Chapter seven explores the use of authentic language samples in language teaching and material design. Issues arising from this approach will be critically discussed, including questions relating to the origin of the data used for teaching and the degree of adaptation of such language samples.

Chapter eight brings together some of the main themes of the book which relate to the use of corpus linguistic methodology in a range of other fields and disciplines. Three further types of corpus-based investigations will be explored, including studies in discourse analysis, pragmatics, and language and culture. The book ends with a summary of some of the challenges that the use of electronic text analysis presents for future research.

Further reading

There are a number of introductory textbooks in corpus linguistics. They tend to vary in focus, particularly with regard to the emphasis placed on technical/methodological issues, and on theory versus application. A very useful introduction that combines the three areas is McEnery and Wilson (2001) and Meyer (2002). Similarly, Kennedy (1998) provides a thorough overview of the field, as well as some detailed discussion of the use of corpus linguistic techniques in the English language teaching context. Another volume that covers both methodological issues and practical applications of corpus research is Biber *et al.* (1998). This publication also includes a separate section with methodology 'boxes' that is presented in an accessible way to readers who are new to the area. McEnery *et al.* (2006) is an accessible advanced resource book for corpus-based language studies. A more technical introduction to corpus building, data manipulation and basic programming can be found in Barnbrook (1996). Sinclair (2005) offers an overview of the nature of corpus research.

There are a range of designated journals that deal with issues related to arts and humanities computing. A particular focus on the exploration of literary texts through electronic text analysis is covered by the journal *Literary and Linguistic Computing*.

Notes

1. See chapter three for different ways of presenting concordance data.
2. CANCODE stands for the Cambridge and Nottingham Corpus of Discourse in English. CANCODE is a five million word corpus of mainly informal naturally occurring conversations and has been developed as a collaborative project between Cambridge University Press and the University of Nottingham. Sole copyright for the corpus resides with Cambridge University Press.
3. See for example Hammond (2002) and Mason (2000) for programming examples for linguistic applications using Java. A number of introductory textbooks on corpus linguistics also have some basic programming examples, such as Barnbrook (1996).
4. See for example David Lee's comprehensive website <http://devoted.to/corpora> for a vast range of links and information in this area.

2   Electronic text resources

Introduction

An electronic text is, in the first instance, a digitally formatted document. Such a document may have been produced in an electronic format, or may have been transferred from a paper copy to electronic media. Transcripts of recorded audio data, e.g. conversations, are electronic texts once they have been entered into digital format. The context in which a text has been produced has both practical and theoretical implications for research projects in this area. On the practical side, the transfer of texts into electronic format can involve a lengthy process of scanning and subsequent editing of the material. Similarly, electronic texts may include elements that cannot easily be handled through textual analysis, such as hyperlinks and images for example. As a result, there are a number of theoretical issues that arise from the transfer of data from one mode into another. These relate mainly to the way in which meaning construction relies on the integrity of a text which can be affected if any of its elements are discarded in the analysis.

The nature of the electronic text resource determines, to a large extent, the research boundaries: a very small collection of texts, for example, would be an inappropriate basis for lexicographical research, simply because it would not contain a sufficient number of instances of a chosen lexical item needed to make any statements about its usage. In the same vein, the nature of the resource also has an impact on the results of a linguistic enquiry, and is therefore tightly linked to the purpose of the study. Thus, the study of a particular lexical item will produce quite different results depending on whether the underlying corpus is a collection of legal documents or a collection of popular newspaper articles. Depending on whether the overall aim of the study is to make statements about the general use of a word or phrase, or whether it relates to the use of a word or phrase in a particular discourse context, a suitable resource has to be found or developed that is either representative of general language use or of use in a restricted context.

Bearing these connections in mind, it has now become common practice to use methods of electronic text analysis to study resources that have not been assembled with a view of representing general language use, but which instead contain the language of a particular author, maybe captured in a single text.

This chapter explores methodological issues involved in using, collecting and assembling electronic text resources for analysis. Starting with some basic principles and choices that underlie the assembly of such resources, the chapter will move on to the description of some contemporary spoken and written corpora, as well as text archives that are currently available to the research community.

What kind of resource for what kind of research?

As outlined above, when we consult or assemble collections of naturally occurring texts for linguistic study, the research purpose dictates the type of resource that we need to consult. Reflecting different research purposes, common distinctions are made between electronic text archives and corpora. The former holds a range of texts and text collections but has not been designed according to particular principles that reflect the purpose of linguistic exploration. Corpora, on the other hand, are designed to represent a particular language variety. Common distinctions are made between *specialized* and *general* corpora, where the former would include texts that belong to a particular type, e.g. academic prose, while the latter would include many different types of texts, often assembled with an aim to produce reference materials such as dictionaries. Other types of corpora include *historical* and *monitor* corpora, *parallel* corpora and *learner* corpora. Historical corpora include texts from different periods of time. One of the most well known historical corpus of English is the *Helsinki corpus* which contains around 1.6 million words from the Old English, Middle English and Early Modern English periods. The design of historical corpora is to some extent restricted by access to different genres, as well as socio-cultural and demographic spread of author origin. This makes it even more important to be explicit about the design criteria and possible effects on analytical results (Rissanen 1989). Historical corpora also allow for the study of language change when compared with corpora from other periods. Monitor corpora can be used for a similar purpose, but focus on current changes in the language. New texts from the same variety are added to the existing corpus at regular intervals, thus contributing to a constantly growing text database. Parallel corpora include texts in at least two languages that have either been directly translated, or produced in different languages for the same purpose. Such corpora are often used for translation studies. Learner corpora contain collections of texts produced by learners of a language. They allow the researcher to identify patterns in a particular variety of learner English and to compare and contrast the language of the learner to that of other users of a language.

A substantial number of different types of corpora are now readily available to researchers, and this chapter will introduce some contemporary resources. At the same time, it is now relatively easy to assemble corpora from scratch for research projects that deal with texts that are available from the internet. An example of such a project would be the analysis of newspaper language, as many newspaper articles are now available online, often in the form of archives that contain substantial amounts of data. Similarly, the analysis of political interviews or policy documents can be facilitated through a corpus of documents drawn from different websites.

When it comes to assembling a corpus for linguistic analysis from scratch or to choosing an existing resource, a number of decisions have to be made that relate mainly to the issues of content and size. These issues are discussed further below.

Corpus size

Existing corpora vary greatly in size, ranging from the one million word corpora developed in the 1960s, such as the *Lancaster-Oslo/Bergen* and the *Brown corpus*, for example, to the *Bank of English*™ corpus, which exceeds 500 million words at the time of writing. The latter is often referred to as a monitor corpus, as new data is added continuously to the resource. The size of a corpus determines, to a large extent, the research possibilities, in particular with regard to analysing patterns of word usage. This is because of the way in which word frequencies are distributed in language. Looking at the frequency list of the top 10 words in the five million-word CANCODE corpus below, we can see that the frequency of individual words drops off sharply as we go down the list. The tenth most frequent word occurs with less than half of the frequency of the most frequent word:

1	THE	156,229
2	I	142,241
3	AND	131,869
4	YOU	128,416
5	IT	99,163
6	TO	98,309
7	A	96,116
8	YEAH	85,497
9	THAT	78,226
10	OF	72,086

Overall, there are 44,167 different words (also called types) that make up the five million-word corpus. Of the 44,167 types, 29,055 types occur with a frequency of only 1. Amongst these low frequency items, which account for around two thirds of the overall number of types, we find words that would intuitively not appear to be infrequent, such as the words *applaud* and *bulky*. Because of this type of distribution, a large corpus is required if the research is concerned with a description of individual lexical items, unless these are drawn from the most frequent words in the language. A larger corpus may ensure that there are enough recurrences of each lexical item to allow for the extraction of patterns that are representative of the language from a concordance output.

However, if we concentrate on the most frequent types in our study then this can be achieved with a smaller corpus. Similarly, the study of common grammatical patterns requires a smaller corpus than the study of common lexical items due to the fact that grammatical patterns are a lot more repetitive than lexical items, and we can therefore expect to find a substantial number of occurrences even in a small corpus. Carter and McCarthy (1995: 43), for example, study spoken grammar in the five million-word CANCODE and argue that this resource is sufficient for the purpose of their research. Overall, however, restrictions on corpus size are often the result of practical considerations, rather than theoretical ones (see Hunston 2002: 26). Thus, when it comes to the extraction of language patterns, it is more desirable to be able to draw on a large amount of data to add to the robustness of the analytical results, but this is often in tension with the practicality of compiling a large corpus, depending on the particular language variety that is being collected.

Another consideration to take on board when it comes to corpus size is the type of analysis that will be used in the exploration of the data. In the social sciences, a distinction is often made between qualitative and quantitative analysis, which at a very basic level relates to the practice of whether or not frequencies form part of the analysis. While corpus linguistics does not necessarily fit comfortably into either of these distinct categories, it is probably fair to say that it has, in the past, tended towards the quantitative paradigm. Thus, the emphasis has been on the extraction of language patterns rather than on the analysis of single occurrences that stand out in any way. In doing so, various techniques for calculating frequencies and attraction between words are used, which will be further discussed in chapter three. Studies that have a quantitative bias necessarily require larger resources.

However, language corpora also form a valuable basis for empirical qualitative research, which focuses on the detailed exploration of particular linguistic choices in context. A general trend towards the use of multi-method approaches to electronic text resources has developed over the past decade and there are now a range of studies which use a quantitative approach as a starting point for a more qualitative subsequent analysis of the output (e.g. O'Keeffe 2004). An example of this process would be a frequency count of all items in a corpus of newspaper articles followed by a more detailed analysis, at text level, of a subset of items that have been isolated from the frequency list on the basis of their relevance to the analysis. This may include the analysis of frequently occurring semantic sets that describe 'war' or 'peace', or the names of political leaders. Such an analysis can provide a way into the data that is informed by the data itself.

Another issue that arises in this context is the length of individual texts in a corpus. In the example above, individual newspaper articles that have been identified may differ in overall length and there might be a temptation to introduce a cut-off point in each document to achieve an equal number of words per document. However, there are various problems associated with this approach, mainly related to the fact that selected parts of any one document are not necessarily a true reflection of the whole document (Sinclair 1991). It is therefore advisable to keep all individual texts in the corpus intact and include them as complete documents.

Corpus content

As with corpus size, the issue of availability of texts also plays a crucial part in the design of the content of the corpus. While certain types of texts, especially those that are generated by using electronic media such as e-mails and word-processed documents, tend to be readily available, others can be more scarce and may require a lengthy collection process and careful manual preparation. Examples of such texts include transcripts of spoken interactions or any documents that are unavailable in electronic format, and which therefore have to be scanned before they can enter a corpus. Despite advances in automatic voice recognition, transcripts of spoken language remain one of the most time-consuming components of modern corpus compilation, which is one of the reasons for the general scarcity of spoken corpora. We will discuss the issue of data preparation in more detail in the next section, but it is worth noting that the level of preparation needed for particular types of texts often influences the choice of content of a corpus. Fortunately, there are now a large number of carefully annotated corpora available to the research community, some of which will be introduced later on in this chapter.

When it comes to the content of a corpus, it is also important to consider the issue of balance. If the aim of the research is to analyse the language of political interviews, for example, a decision would have to be made as to the amount of data that can be feasibly collected from different types of political interviews to be representative of the genre as a whole. How many interviews would have to be drawn from TV news programmes versus those that are reported in newspapers or other written media? How many interviews should be conducted by male versus female interviewers and should any interviews be included that involve more than two speakers? Is a representation of different types of politicians required and if so what is the basis of the categories?

How do we know that the texts that we have selected to represent a particular genre are truly representative? After all, we can only really achieve a representative sample if we know the consistency of the total number of texts from which our sample is drawn (see Hunston 2002: 28). This is a particular problem for genres that are not habitually recorded in any form. For example, it is almost impossible to argue that we can ever assemble a corpus that is representative of casual conversation, since we cannot know what the entire production of this genre, even in a single day in a particular language variety, might look like. However, even with text sources that are recorded, we do not always know the exact consistency of the resource.

One way of addressing the issue of representativeness is to collect a proportional sample. For example, you could record all of the political interviews that are broadcast on all the major TV channels in one day or week, and then explain the different proportions according to this sampling technique. However, if the aim is to contrast a particular type of political interview, say one that is conducted by a male interviewer versus one that is conducted by a female interviewer, then it would make sense to collect an equal number of interviews in the respective categories. The sampling method thus depends, to a large extent, on the research question. Note that in either case the design criteria for such a corpus should be external to the texts, relating to the use of language in a recognized context that exists outside the realm of language analysis (see Sinclair 2005). If the texts were chosen according to text internal criteria, such as the frequency of modal verbs for example, the analysis would be self-fulfilling to a large extent in that we would expect the comparison of linguistic patterns to support the distinctions made at the stage of text selection.

There are certain types of electronic text collections of which we do know the overall picture, including their number of words, date of origin, text-types, etc. Take, for example, a corpus of Shakespeare's writings, or even a corpus of your own academic essays (see Coniam 2004). These are finite text collections that are representative of the writing of a particular author in a particular genre, and they can be explored with the use of electronic text analysis. However, the types of analyses that can be carried out on the basis of such texts are limited to their immediate context, and don't allow us to make any general statements about a language variety. They do, however, offer a framework for description of the style of an author as used in a particular genre. Such text collections blur the distinction between text archives and corpora as the design criteria are pre-determined to a large extent.

Theories of representativeness of language in use are still in need of further development and there are different arguments for the inclusion of different size samples from particular sources in a corpus (see Biber 1993). In the absence of refined models and frameworks in this area, it is therefore important to be explicit about the criteria and thinking that have influenced corpus design decisions, and to evaluate any analytical results in light of those decisions.

From text to corpus: stages of handling electronic texts

There are basically three processes involved in handling electronic text collections; data collection, annotation and mark-up, and storage. We have already discussed the corpus collection and design stage, so in this section we will concentrate on data representation and storage. There are various ways of preparing a digitized document or collection of documents and this process not only influences the scope of the analysis of a particular text but also the nature of the text itself. The latter applies in particular to texts that have been annotated with various hyper-links. Text corpora traditionally consist of text only and there is currently no easy way of integrating the different layers of texts provided through hyperlinks into the standard software tools for analysing corpus resources. This may well change in the future as the internet is becoming a more prominent resource for corpus linguists.

In order to make a text usable and reusable for the wider research community it has become common practice to add additional information to the text. This information takes the form of 'mark-up' and 'annotation'.

Mark-up

Mark-up is the process of adding consistent codes to a text which contain informa-tion about its typography and layout. This may include speaker codes in a transcript of spoken data or codes that mark headings or new paragraphs in a written docu-ment. There are various mark-up systems currently in use, including SGML (Standard Generalized Mark-up Language) and the related XML (Extensible Mark-up Language). These act as a meta-language, which is any language or terminology that is used to describe another language, here used to give additional information about textual features. Both have been adopted by the TEI (*Text Encoding Initiative*), a recognized body that aims to ensure a consistent use of particular coding systems.

Mark-up of texts can aid the automatic or electronic processing of textual fea-tures. The mark-up of individual speakers in a spoken corpus, for example, allows for a targeted analysis of different speakers or of one particular speaker. The stan-dard way of representing mark-up information is through angle brackets, such as in the following list of some of the codes that are used in *The Freiburg–Brown Corpus of American* English:[1]

<p_>	begin paragraph
<p/>	end paragraph
<h_>	begin headline
<h/>	end headline
<h|>	one word headline
<quote_>	begin quotation
<quote/>	end quotation
<quote|>	one word quotation
<tf_>	begin typeface change
<tf/>	end typeface change
<tf|>	one word typeface change
<*_><*/>	begin/end unusable character

<foreign_> begin foreign words
end foreign words
<foreign|> one foreign word

Similarly, the following extract from the CANCODE spoken corpus contains specific mark-up language used to identify speakers and extralinguistic phenomena such as pauses:[2]

<$1> That's right. Er why do you think Twelve's treated differently?
<$E> *pause* <\$E> Why do you think+
<$4> Erm.

In this short extract of conversation from the *CANCODE* corpus we see that the extralinguistic information *pause* is marked by a particular code in angle brackets, <$E> and <\$E>, on either side of the word. It is worth noting that while tagging conventions differ, the most commonly used way in which individual phenomena are marked-up is by using a set of angle brackets that consist of an opening tag with an indentifier symbol, number or letter, and a closing tag which contains the same identifier usually preceded by a forward slash as in <head> </head>.

Most data processing software can be set to ignore all information in angle brackets and thus disregard any mark-up information. The amount of mark-up information required depends on the overall purpose of the analysis.

Annotation

Analytical information that is added to a text is often referred to as 'annotation'. Texts can be annotated automatically by a software program, or in a semi-automated or manual manner depending on the type of annotation that is being used. Annotation is often represented with the use of codes that follow the format of mark-up codes, outlined above. In terms of literary texts, annotation can preserve different interpretations of individual passages or words in a digital format. This can be extremely useful to the research community not only because it aids the preservation of different types of analysis and makes the interpretative processes more explicit, but also because it enables the comparison of different interpretations, either in a manual or sometimes in an automated manner.

Depending on the type of research question you are seeking to address, you may need to carry out your own annotations manually. These may include the annotation of particular speech acts in a corpus or different forms of speech and thought presentation in literary discourse, which will be expanded on in Chapter five (see also Semino and Short 2004).

In the area of corpus linguistics, the process of annotation is closely related to the processes of 'tagging' or 'parsing' of texts. The former is a code added to each word in a text and identifies which Part Of Speech (POS) individual words represent, while the latter assigns functional categories on the basis of this POS information.

Programs for automated POS annotation are now widely available and highly accurate in the POS categories they assign to each word.[3] Other types of automated annotation, including those that identify functional elements and word senses, are currently being developed. Below is an example of a speaker turn in the CANCODE corpus that has been annotated for POS:

> And [Cand] the [Dthe] security [Nsg] guard [Nsg] was [VFpastBe] walking [VPpres] about [T] checking [VPpres] everything [Pind] was [VFpastBe] okay [Jbas] and [Cand] and [Cand] then...

Key: [Jbas] adjective, base; [Nsg] noun, singular; [Cand] conjunction, coordinating; [Dthe] definite article; [Nsg] noun, singular; [VFpastBe] verb, finite, past; [VPpres] verb, particle, present; [Pind] pronoun, indefinite.

A POS tagged corpus allows for a search of lexical items in a particular grammatical role, as well as for a sequence that contains both grammatical categories and lexical items, which will be illustrated further in chapter four. In a tagged corpus, a search of the word *play* can thus be further specified to include only those instances where *play* is used as a noun rather than as a verb, as in the concordance lines taken from *CANCODE* below:

> [Nsg] he [Ppers] had [VFpastHave] a [Da] **play** [Nsg] run [Nsg] in [T] the [Dthe] West [Nsg] En
> we [Ppers] have [VFpresHave] a [Da] **play** [Nsg] with [T] with [T] the [Dthe] children [Npl]
> We [Ppers] did [VFpast] a [Da] **play** [Nsg] scheme [Nsg] with T] the [Dthe] infants
> ave] got [VPpast] to [T] a [Da] **play** [Nsg] in [T] the [Dthe] careers [Npl]
> [Ppers] saw [VFpast] a [Da] a [Da] **play** [Nsg] but [Cand] obviously [A] because [C] it

While it is possible to keep the POS tags in a separate file and display only the plain text for purposes of analysis, the concordance lines above highlight the potential intrusiveness of tags when it comes to reading individual concordance lines. There are a number of applications that require tags and other types of annotation. In order to minimize the interference with the text, and to facilitate the reusability of the resource, it is advisable to keep plain text documents separate from the tagged versions and to put as much effort as possible into the documentation of the annotation process.

In terms of linguistic annotation, such as POS tagging or the annotation of other categories, the degree of analytical intervention with the data at the stage of representation is worth bearing in mind. While the type of information added through annotation can be extremely useful in the context of particular corpus projects,

Sinclair (2004a: 190–1) argues that it may interfere with the data in a way that makes it difficult to read concordance outputs and recognize patterns, and may also introduce an analytical bias into the data, which reinforces the categories imposed through the annotation system.

The question of data representation is an important one for corpus linguistics. As new technologies for the representation, annotation and alignment of different data streams, such as audio and visual, become available, it will be a key task for the field to develop an understanding of how analytical techniques – whether they are automated or not – implicated in the organization of corpora themselves affect emerging description, theory and practice. It is inevitable that the decisions we take, with regard to the mark-up and annotation of corpora, will have some impact on the results of our analysis. A spoken corpus that includes the annotation of over-lapping speech, for example, will generate different results in a study of turn boundaries than one that does not include such annotation. At the same time, we have to recognize that the annotation of overlaps in speech is a messy task in itself and if carried out manually might produce different results depending on different researchers tasked with the coding. This may then mean that the study becomes dif-ficult to replicate. The general standards and guidelines introduced by bodies such as the *NERC* and *TEI* are therefore aimed partly at making corpus resources reusable by the research community.

Metadata

A third type of information that is used in the representation of electronic texts is metadata.[4] Metadata is 'data about data' and tends to contain information about the content, source, quality and other characteristics of a particular text. This data can be useful when the corpus is shared and reused by the community and also assists in the preservation of electronic texts. Metadata can be kept in a separate database or included as a 'header' at the start of each document (usually encoded though mark-up language). A separate database with this information makes it easier to compare different types of documents and has the distinct advantage that it can be further extended by other users of the same data. The following is an example of metadata relating to a header element taken from the *Text Encoding Initiative* website.[5] The metadata in this particular example provides further infor-mation about the source of the text:

```
<encodingDesc>
<projectDesc>
<p>Texts were collected to illustrate the full range of twentieth-century
spoken and written Swedish, written by native Swedish authors.</p>
</projectDesc>
<samplingDecl>
```

```
<p>Sample of 2000 words taken from the beginning of the text.</p>
</samplingDecl>
<editorialDecl>
<interpretation>
<p>Errors in transcription controlled by using the SUC spell checker,
v.2.4</p>
</interpretation>
</editorialDecl>
</encodingDesc>
```

The information encoded in the metadata above includes reference to the overall aim of the project in that the text in question was 'collected to illustrate the full range of 20th century spoken and written Swedish, written by native Swedish authors'. Other tags used in this set such as <samplingDecl>, <editorialDecl>, and <refsDecl> give further information on sampling and other editorial processes applied to the text.

This type of information is invaluable when other people come to use a particular electronic text resource. The documentation of the design rationale, as well as the various editorial processes that an individual text has been subjected to during the collection and archiving stages, allows other researchers to assess its suitability for their own research purposes.

The representation of spoken data

One of the biggest challenges in corpus linguistic research is probably the representation of spoken data, which is why a separate section is set aside for discussing this issue here. There is no doubt that the collection of spoken language is far more labourious than the collection of written samples, but the richness of this type of data can make the extra effort worthwhile. Unscripted, naturally occurring conversations can be particularly interesting for the study of spoken grammar and lexis, and for the analysis of the construction of meaning in interaction (McCarthy 1998, Carter 2004, Halliday 2004). However, the representation of spoken data is a major issue in this context, as the recorded conversations have to undergo a transition from the spoken mode to the written before they can be included in a corpus. In transcribing spoken discourse we have to make various choices as to the amount of detail we wish to include in the written record. Since there are so many layers of detail that carry meaning in spoken interaction, this task can easily become a black hole (McCarthy 1998: 13) with a potentially infinite amount of contextual information to record (Cook 1990). The reason for this is that spoken interaction is essentially multi-modal in nature, featuring a careful interplay between textual, prosodic and gestural elements in the construction of meaning. In terms of individual projects it is therefore important to decide exactly on the purpose of the study and what type of transcription is needed. It is advisable to identify the spoken feature of interest at the outset and to tailor the focus of the transcription accordingly. For example, a study of discourse structure might require the transcription to include overlaps but not detailed prosodic information.

The level of detail required for transcribing spoken discourse very much depends on the overall research question. It is important to document the steps in transcribing spoken data carefully, and to discuss any emerging results against the backdrop of the chosen conventions. There are now a number of different types of transcription conventions available, including those adopted by the *Network of European Reference Corpora (NERC)*, which was used for the spoken component of the *COBUILD* project (Sinclair 1987). This transcription system contains four layers, ranging from basic orthographic representation to very detailed transcription, including information about prosody.

Another set of guidelines for transcribing spoken data has been recommended by the *TEI* and has been applied, for example, to the *British National Corpus*. These guidelines include the representation of structural, contextual, prosodic, temporal and kinesic elements of spoken interactions and provide a useful resource for the transcription of different levels of detail required to meet particular research goals.

The level of detail of transcription reflects the basic needs of the type of research that they are intended to inform. One of the corpora that has been transcribed to a particularly advanced level of detail is the *London-Lund Corpus*. Alongside the standard encoding of textual structure, speaker turns and overlaps, this corpus also includes prosodic information and has remained a valuable resource for a wide range of researchers.

Recent advances in the representation and alignment of different data streams have started to provide possibilities for studying spoken discourse in an integrated framework including textual, prosodic and video data.[6] The alignment of the different elements and the software needed to analyse such a multi-modal resource are still in the early stages of development, and at the present time it would probably be beyond the scope of the majority of individual corpus projects to develop a searchable resource that includes representation of all of these three data streams.

Storage

The last stage in the handling process of electronic texts is that of storage, which includes considerations of data access for other users. Most text collections can be stored in the form of a number of different text files in a folder on a standard PC. As discussed above, if a text or text collection includes extensive annotation, it can be useful to store the data both in plain text format and in annotated format, but to keep the two versions separate. Software packages that have been designed to manipulate and analyse corpus data can be used to access different locations of files and folders stored on a PC.

Electronic text analysis lends itself to collaborative research, as most texts can now be exchanged relatively easily between users via file transfer protocols. This ease of access allows for replication as well as extension of research in this area. With the development of technologies that promote collaborative data analysis via distributed computational infrastructures, an increasing number of users are now able to access and share large amounts of natural language in text, sound and video format.

Contemporary electronic text resources

As discussed at the beginning of this chapter, there are different types of text corpora that are associated with different research aims. Apart from the range of different corpora that have undergone a principled design process to reflect the context of a given research question, there are other types of electronic resources that have not been assembled explicitly for linguistic study, such as the world-wide web and text archives. Both are useful resources for linguistic study, but the internet is primarily used for information transfer and text archives tend to be assembled to preserve texts rather than to explore them linguistically (see Hunston 2002: 2). The design principles underlying these resources are different to those that apply to a corpus, especially as regards the sampling process. It is therefore important to be explicit about the origin of the resource and to acknowledge the potential effect of the nature of the data on the analytical results.

Access to existing electronic text resources is widely available. Contemporary corpora are distributed in a variety of formats including CD-ROMs and online archives. Some existing corpora can be downloaded from the internet free of charge while others can be consulted on a sample basis and require the payment of a fee for use of the full resource. Many new corpora are being assembled every year for particular research projects, and there is a growing number of initiatives that are concerned with the preservation, management and distribution of corpora and electronic texts in general. At the same time, there is an increasing number of publishers who make available electronic editions of major literary works on a commercial basis.

The remainder of this chapter will introduce some of the resources that have been used extensively in language and literary research. Within the scope of this publication such a list cannot be exhaustive and thus focuses on those resources that are of relevance to the issues discussed in this book, with a further emphasis on those that are freely accessible. The companion website contains links to all individual electronic text projects mentioned below. The website provides information on the type of access that is available for these resources, as well as further information on other resources that cannot be covered here due to space limitations. All websites that are mentioned throughout this book are also included in the bibliography of websites.

Early corpora

When it comes to the history of corpus design a distinction is often made between first and second-generation corpora. First generation corpora are generally those that were developed in the 1950s, 1960s and 1970s. These corpora were often limited in size with a one million-word threshold. The relatively small size of these collections is partly a reflection of the technological possibilities at the time.

One of the first corpora to be developed in electronic format is the *London-Lund Corpus* (LLC), which contains just over half a million words of spoken text recorded between the mid-1950s and the mid-1980s. The texts, which are prosodically transcribed, were collected at the *Survey of English Usage* (SEU) at University College London (see Svartvik 1990). Two other first generation corpora designed in the 1960s and 1970s are the *Brown Corpus* and the *Lancaster-Oslo/Bergen* corpus. Both corpora are based on the same design, including 500 samples of text of 2000 words each. The *Brown Corpus* is based on American written English, while the *Lancaster-Oslo/Bergen* corpus consists of written British English. These two corpora have been particularly used for the comparison between British and American English and both corpora can be accessed and searched online. Corpora of other varieties of English have been developed based on essentially the same design as the original *Brown Corpus*, including *The Kolhapur Corpus* of Indian English, *The Wellington Corpus* of written New Zealand English, and *The Australian Corpus* of English.

In the 1990s two updated versions of the *Brown* and the *Lancaster-Oslo/Bergen Corpus* were developed which included contemporary text samples. These corpora followed the same design as their two predecessors and are referred to as the *Freiburg-LOB Corpus of British English* (FLOB) and, as already discussed above, the *Freiburg-Brown Corpus of American English* (FROWN). They can be used as a basis for diachronic comparisons with the original *Brown* and *LOB* corpora. Many of the first generation corpora, including the ones mentioned above, are available on CD-ROM as part of *The International Computer Archive of Modern and Medieval English*.

Second-generation corpora

Large corpora

Two of the most substantial corpus projects developed in the 1980s and 1990s are the *Collins and Birmingham University International Language Database* (COBUILD) and the *British National Corpus*. Both offer a valuable resource for the study of everyday spoken and written English.

The *COBUILD* corpus, which is also referred to as the *Bank of English*™, was developed in the 1990s as a monitor corpus. This means that new texts are constantly being added to this database and at the time of writing the overall size of the corpus exceeds 500,000 million words. One of the main aims of this project has been to provide a textual database for the compilation of dictionaries and lexicography research. The corpus contains samples of both British and American written language, as well as transcribed speech from interviews, broadcast and conversation. Access to a corpus concordance sampler, which includes 56 million words of the overall corpus, is provided via a website.[7] The sampler web interface also allows you to search for collocations and to add POS tags and wildcards to your search word.

The *British National Corpus* (BNC) was assembled by a consortium of British publishers, of academic institutions including Oxford University Computing services, Lancaster University's Centre for Computer Research on the English language and the British Library. Compiled in the late 1980s and early 1990s it is now a 100 million-word corpus of modern British English, consisting of 90 per cent written and 10 per cent spoken language (including speeches, meetings, lectures and some casual conversation). The BNC offers an online search facility that displays a limited number of random instances of a word or phrase.[8]

Apart from these two major corpora, many publishing houses have developed their own corpora that serve as a resource for authors, mainly in the area of lexicography. These include the 30 million-word *Longman Corpus Network* and the 600 million word *Cambridge International Corpus*.

Another large corpus project is the *International Corpus of English* (ICE), which was initiated in 1990 as a resource for comparing different varieties of English. The overall aim of this project is to collect corpora of one million word written and spoken English in 20 different varieties. A number of the different components have now been completed and some of these, including the British component, can currently be downloaded from the relevant websites.[9]

Specialized corpora and electronic text resources

When a corpus has been designed to capture the language of a particular domain rather than the language in general, it is often called a specialized corpus. Contemporary specialized corpora range from those that represent the language of a particular group of people, to those that represent a particular mode of discourse.

Some of the major developments of specialized corpora have taken place in the domain of academic discourse. The *Michigan Corpus of Academic Spoken English* (MICASE), for example, includes over 1.8 million words of carefully transcribed spoken discourse in academic settings. These include, among others, lectures, presentations, seminars, tutorials and office hours. The corpus can be accessed via a website, which features a user-friendly interface that facilitates a variety of different types of searches. The British counterpart to the MICASE is the *British Academic Spoken English corpus* (BASE). The design and mark-up of this corpus are set to mirror that of MICASE to facilitate comparisons across the two varieties.

Since specialized corpora tend to be built for the exploration of a particular discourse domain, there can be a greater need to assemble these resources from scratch in order for them to meet the requirements of a particular research project. With the advent of the internet, many specialized corpora can be assembled relatively quickly. An exploration of media discourse, for example, can be facilitated by the development of a corpus that consists of texts from the many newspaper and interview websites that are now available. Many newspapers store their texts in archives that can be accessed, often free of charge. Similarly, spoken and written texts of political discourse, as well as policy documents can be accessed via the internet and brought together as a corpus. And even the analysis of discourse that is not normally kept in the public domain, such as medical discourse, can sometimes be accessed online.[10]

Learner corpora

Chapter seven will deal with the impact of electronic text analysis in the area of English language teaching but we will briefly consider here the use of learner corpora. The development of learner corpora, i.e. collections of language samples produced by individuals who are learners of the respective language, has played a major part in this context. The analysis of such data makes it possible to track developmental aspects of learner language, as well as highlight particular areas of difficulty for the learner based on comparisons with the language used by native speakers. At the same time, learner corpora can be used as a basis for better descriptions of different varieties that emerge when non-native speakers communicate. The design criteria for learner corpora have a slightly different focus to native speaker corpora in that particular emphasis has to be placed on the level of consistency of the resource in terms of the language background of the speakers, including their level of proficiency and first language. With these key variables controlled, it is relatively straightforward to assemble a small learner corpus, such as a corpus of student compositions for example.

The scope of analysing learner data when it comes to the design of reference works and other teaching materials is substantial, and it is therefore not surprising that many contemporary learner corpora are developed by publishing houses. These include the 15 million-word *Cambridge Learner Corpus of written English* and the 10 million word *Longman Learners' Corpus of written English*. However, such resources are not usually accessible to researchers, unless they are also authors for the respective publishing houses.

One of the key places for research into learner language is the *Centre for English Corpus Linguistics* at the University of Louvain in Belgium. One of the projects developed at this centre is the *International Corpus of Learners' English* (ICLE), a two million-word corpus which consists mainly of academic writing produced by students from different mother-tongue backgrounds. A further development of a spoken learner corpus is currently underway at the same centre. Another example of a spoken learner corpus is the *Vienna-Oxford International Corpus of English* (VOICE), which is currently being developed at Vienna University and supported by Oxford University Press. The VOICE project is based on the use of English as a lingua franca, that is in context where English is chosen as a language of communication between speakers with different first languages (Seidlhofer 2002).[11]

Literary corpora and electronic text resources

There are a number of distribution archives that provide access to electronic versions of literary texts including, for example, *Project Gutenberg* and the *Oxford Text Archive*.

These initiatives prepare and store electronic texts and provide tools for their analysis to support a large research community. The main aim tends to be the preservation of text resources and the development of integrated digital infra-structures to enable individual and collaborative research that is resource intensive. Electronic text archives are developed for a purpose that is different to the one that tends to underlie the construction of language corpora. Kennedy (1998: 57) makes the following distinction between archives and corpora:

> In a general sense, databases are collections of information which are designed to facilitate data entry and retrieval. Linguistic corpora, at one extreme, are a subset of databases which have been designed and structured specifically to be used for linguistic description and analysis. Archives, at the other extreme, are usually unstructured repositories of texts.

An example of a text archive is the *Oxford Text Archive* (OTA) mentioned above. The *Oxford Text Archive* is part of the Arts and Humanities Data Service and has as its main aim to 'collect, catalogue, and preserve high-quality electronic texts for research and teaching'.[12] At the time of writing, the OTA distributes in excess of 2500 resources in over 25 different languages. Their website, which is freely accessible, allows users to search the extended catalogue of holdings using a key word in context search facility. Due to copyright restrictions, it tends to be more difficult to gain access to electronic versions of modern literary texts. In such instances it is worth contacting the publisher to ascertain whether an electronic version can be made available for research purposes.

A focus on providing tools and resources for the electronic analysis of literary and non-literary texts can be found in TAPOR. The *Text-Analysis Portal for Research* is a collaborative project between a number of Canadian Universities which aims to provide a gateway for electronic texts and text analysis tools.[13] It is split into a number of local centres which all have an individual research focus in this area and which will eventually combine to a co-ordinated portal for the study of electronic texts. Current centre projects include a wide variety of approaches to digital texts, ranging from annotated Shakespeare editions to digitized collections of audio-taped interviews.

Such initiatives facilitate access to language resources by a large community of researchers and provide tools to search, retrieve, categorize and manipulate documents and collections of documents of natural language.

The web as corpus

As outlined in chapter one, we would not normally refer to the web as a corpus mainly because there are no explicit design criteria on which this vast collection of texts is based. Since we do not know the overall consistency of the body of texts that a search engine explores, it is difficult to make any statements about the output of such searches in terms of their representativeness of a particular language variety, other than the variety of the 'language of the internet', which may not be consistent from one day to the next. Even if we did know the broad categories into which different internet texts would fall, we may not be able to determine their origin, thus losing important contextual information such as the first language of the author for example. In addition, the consistency of the texts themselves may mean that a purely textual analysis might be problematic. This is because many texts on the internet use hyperlinks and images as part of their meaning construction (see Sinclair 2005). As pointed out above, these require a multi-modal approach for their analysis. However, the world wide web can provide us with interesting and up-to-date information about language in use, including new word creations.

There are a number of *search engines* that will return searches for individual lexical items and phrases in a Key Word in Context format. User-friendly interfaces to facilitate this type of search have been developed including that of the *WebCorp project* (see Renouf *et al.* 2004). This interface allows users to specify a search word, phrase or pattern (using wildcards) and to further specify the domain of discourse on which the search will be based. Thus it is possible to restrict the search, for example to particular newspapers, which makes it possible to delineate some design criteria for the corpus on which the search is based, and to move from a relatively broad definition of the web as corpus to a narrower specialized corpus. Further specifications are possible, including the search for collocations and the definition of a time frame during which the searched pages have last been modified. This allows a diachronic search of internet texts. The output is comprehensively structured and includes information about the texts that have been searched, as well as links to the source texts of each concordance line. The *WebCorp* interface can also be used to generate frequency lists of websites specified by the user. It is clearly a valuable resource to use in its own right but can also be used to complement research on finite corpora in terms of the up-to-date evidence of language in use that it can offer (see Kübler 2004).

Summary

This chapter has focused on the description of general processes involved in corpus design, data representation and storage, and has given an overview of contemporary electronic text resources. After reading this chapter you should be able to make a decision on whether you need to develop your own corpus to address a particular research question and, if so, how you go about doing this. In addition, this chapter has provided on overview of some existing corpora that you might draw on. Since electronic text analysis is such a fast moving field, with new corpora being developed every year, a simple search via any of the standard internet search engines will always reveal additional and new resources in the field. Having outlined issues and practices in the design and development of electronic text resources, the next chapter will focus on different kinds of techniques and programs that can be used to analyse them.

Activities

1. Design your own electronic text resource to address a particular research question. In doing so, follow the steps below:
    - Identify your research question and make a decision about the size and content of your resource that is likely to be required to address your particular research question.
    - Set your external design criteria and assess the feasibility of collecting data according to these criteria, revise your decision where necessary, and document the rationale behind your decisions.
    - Identify texts that may be used to assemble your resource, and assess any copyright or other restrictions for using those texts for research purposes.
    - Decide on a sampling technique and document the rationale for this, as well as the sampling process itself.
    - Assemble your resource and store it as text files on your computer. In chapter three various ways of analysing your resource will be discussed.
2. Have a go at using some of the text resources discussed in this chapter. You will find relevant web-links both on the companion website and in the bibliogra-

phy of websites. Are any of the online resources that are freely accessible sufficient to address the research question you have identified in 1? If not, can they be adapted? And what kinds of processes would this involve?

Further reading

The most relevant reading for this chapter can be done by visiting the individual websites that have been mentioned, and by making yourself familiar with the various descriptions of the respective resources that have been discussed. *A Guide to Good Practice* in developing linguistic corpora edited by Martin Wynne has recently been made available on the internet (<http://www.ahds.ac.uk/creating/guides/linguistic-corpora/index.htm>). This guide provides a collection of practical papers on a wide range of issues in corpus design and annotation.

There are a number of further books and articles that deal with issues of corpus design such as Hunston (2002, particularly chapter two) and Biber (1993). In terms of annotation of corpus resources, there are a range of edited volumes that cover a variety of issues in this area including Garside *et al.* (1997) and Leech *et al.* (1995). Further information about the analytical implications of different transcription systems can be found in McCarthy (1998) and Cook (1990). Thompson (2005) discusses a range of issues related to the development of spoken language corpora.

Notes

1. Codes for the The Freiburg – Brown Corpus of American English can be accessed at: <http://khnt.hit.uib.no/icame/manuals/frown/CODE.HTM>.
2. Please see Appendix 1 for CANCODE transcription conventions used for the remainder of this book.
3. See for example CLAWS (the Constituent Likelihood Automatic Word-tagging System) developed at UCREL at Lancaster University which has been used to tag the British National Corpus: <http://www.comp.lancs.ac.uk/computing/research/ucrel/claws/>.
4. The term *metadata* is sometimes used as an umbrella term to include analytical and editorial annotation of texts. Burnard (2005) for example distinguishes between editorial, analytic, descriptive and administrative metadata. However, for the purpose of this book the term metadata has been used only to refer to descriptive and administrative information added to a text.
5. TEI website accessed 6 June 2005: <http://www.tei-c.org/P5/Guidelines/SH.html> This version has been revised and re-edited by Syd Bauman and Lou Burnard.
6. See for example the work carried out at the Max Planck Institute for psycholinguistics at <http://www.mpi.nl/corpus/> and at the National Centre for e-Social Science at <http://www.ncess.ac.uk/nodes/digitalrecord>.
7. The Cobuild corpus concordance and collocation sampler is available at <http://www.collins.co.uk/Corpus/CorpusSearch.aspx>.

8. The BNC online simple search facility can be accessed at <http://sara.natcorp. ox.ac.uk/lookup.html>.

9. More information on availability can be found on the main website of the ICE corpus: <http://www.ucl.ac.uk/english-usage/ice/index.htm>.

10. An example of medical discourse is the Database of Individual Patient Experiences (DIPEx) at <http://www.dipex.org/>. Please note that permission for extracting, analysing and quoting data from any archive or website must be cleared with the relevant copyright holders.

11. According to Barbara Seidlhofer (personal communication) there are plans to make this resource widely accessible for research purposes.

12. Oxford Text Archive website <http://ota.ox.ac.uk/>. Accessed on 25 July 2005.

13. The TAPoR website can be accessed at <http://tapor.ca>.

3 Exploring frequencies in texts: basic techniques

Introduction

This chapter moves from the discussion of design and development of electronic text resources to techniques and practices in data analysis. The particular focus of this chapter will be on the quantitative exploration of texts and text collections, and, as such, it will be mainly concerned with the role of frequencies in individual texts and in comparisons between different texts. In this context, the chapter will discuss different types of wordlists and ways in which they can be used for contrastive studies of different texts. The analysis of individual lexical items and phrases will be discussed further in chapter four.

There are three main ways in which the techniques outlined in this chapter and in the next chapter can inform the research process:

- **Generating hypotheses**. Wordlists of individual texts can highlight items that are characteristic for a particular domain, author or text-type. Similarly, the analysis of keywords, i.e. those words that occur with a significantly higher or lower frequency in a text in relation to another body of text, can be useful to establish an initial characterization of a particular type of discourse. As such, frequency lists can inform the generation of hypotheses and research questions pertaining to a particular domain of discourse, which can be further explored with the use of other methods.
- **Testing hypotheses**. In many cases electronic text analysis is used to test existing hypotheses in any area that deals with the use of language. In sociolinguistic studies this process might be related to the use of a linguistic variable in relation to a social variable. In English language teaching it may relate to the usage of a particular grammatical construction in spoken discourse that is not covered by traditional textbooks, and that might be difficult to describe fully on the basis of intuition alone. In the analysis of literary texts it might relate to a question of authorial style and choice of words that relate to particular semantic fields. In political science it may be

the comparison of linguistic devices used by different political parties, for example in the context of election campaign discourse. In all of these cases, the techniques are used to test a hypothesis that may have been formed without reference to the particular texts that will be used to test it.

- **Facilitating manual processes**. Some processes of text analysis that have traditionally been carried out manually can be automated with the use of the techniques introduced in the next two chapters. This includes the extraction of frequency information of individual words and phrases, as well as the representation of individual instances in a concordance output. Such processes do not necessarily have to be motivated by a particular research question but may simply be used as ways of representing different features of a text, possibly as a resource for future exploration by other researchers.

Tognini-Bonelli (2001) uses the terms *corpus-driven* and *corpus-based* in relation to the processes of generating and testing hypotheses. These processes can be iterative and are facilitated by using suitable software and text resources.

Once a suitable electronic text resource has been identified or assembled, and possibly annotated from scratch, it can be explored further with the use of some basic techniques in text manipulation. Before we consider a few of these techniques in more detail, the following section gives a brief overview of some of the software resources that can be used to facilitate this process.

Software packages

There are currently a number of user-friendly software packages available which facilitate the manipulation and analysis of electronic texts. Common functionalities include the generation of frequency counts according to specified criteria, comparisons of frequency information in different texts, different formats of concordance outputs, including the Key Word In Context (KWIC) concordance, and the extraction of multi-word units or clusters of items in a text. Many of these programs can be downloaded from the internet or used directly via an interactive website. The *Compleat Lexical Tutor*, developed by Tom Cobb, for example, provides a user-friendly interface that can currently be used free of charge via the internet. The interactive website, which was developed as a resource for data-driven learning, enables the generation of frequency lists of your own files, as well as of some stored samples of electronic text collections. It can also be used to run concordances, extract phrases, generate vocabulary profiles, and develop teaching material based on corpus data. Another example of a software package that can currently be accessed via the internet is *View: Variation in English Words and Phrases* developed by Mark Davies. This user-friendly interface facilitates a comparison of words and phrases in different registers in the British National Corpus.

Other programs are distributed commercially, often by publishing houses, and can be purchased for a fee, such as *Wordsmith Tools* developed by Mike Scott for example. Some programs are tied to a particular resource and can only be used with the resources that they have been designed for. The choice of which software package to use is dependent on the overall research aim, and influenced by the scope of different programs. There are now too many different programs available for it to be feasible to review them within the remit of this publication. However, a number of relevant websites are listed in the bibliography of websites and on the companion website.

For those with some basic programming knowledge, there is also the possibility to write their own software for text manipulation. However, given the introductory nature of this book, the remainder of the chapter will concentrate on the use of available software packages in the exploration of electronic texts, rather than on programming examples and the particular algorithms associated with them.

Basic information about the text

Most software packages that allow textual data to be sorted into concordance outputs also have a facility that produces some basic information about the text or collection of texts you want to study. This information can include average sentence length, word length, number of paragraphs, number of individual running words (also called tokens) and number of different words (also called types), number of lexical items and number of grammatical items (in tagged corpora).

Type-token ratio

Some of the information above can be expressed in terms of ratios, such as the ratio between grammatical and lexical items in the text, which is also referred to as lexical density. A more common ratio, that is often calculated in order to gain some basic understanding of the lexical variation within the text, is the *type-token* ratio. As mentioned above, the term *tokens* refers to the number of running words in a text while the term *types* refers to the number of different words. As an example, consider the first sentence of this chapter:

> This chapter moves from the discussion of design and development of electronic text resources to techniques and practices in data analysis.

This sentence contains 21 tokens and 19 types as the word *and* and the word *of* occur twice. The type-token ratio is calculated by dividing the number of tokens in a text by the number of types, so the type-token ratio for the above sentence would be $21/19 = 1.11$. This kind of information can be useful when assessing the level of complexity of a particular text or text collection, for example in comparisons between documents written for different types of audiences. As a general rule the higher the type-token ratio the less varied the text. However, the problem with the calculation of type-token ratios is that they are dependent on the overall size of the text(s) on which they are based. It is thus advisable only to compare type-token ratios of text(s) of similar length.

While information about type-token ratios, as well as sentence and word length, can provide some insight into the level of complexity of a text, a closer linguistic analysis of grammatical structure and semantic fields of the individual items that occur is necessary to make any robust statements about textual complexity. However, the basic calculations discussed here can be used as a starting point for more elaborate types of analysis and as elements that contribute to the overall picture of a text that emerges through quantitative and qualitative kinds of analysis.

Word lists

Single words

One important insight into language use that has become possible through electronic text analysis is the derivation of frequency information of individual lexical items and phrases. The frequency of a word or phrase in different text types is an important part of its description in the context of use. This aspect is also important in areas of application such as English language teaching for example, where it has become possible to use raw frequency information and distribution to inform material design. Various word lists exist in the ELT context, which are based to some degree on word frequency in a corpus, such as the *Academic Word List* (Coxhead 2000) for example. Wordlists also provide a general picture of a text or collection of texts, and are a good starting point for subsequent searches of individual items at the concordance level. In addition, word lists are useful resources for comparing different corpora, such as those that represent spoken versus written discourse, or American versus British English for example.

Wordlists can be generated by counting the number of identical items in a corpus. This can be done on the basis of frequency order, alphabetical order, in lemmatized format and according to grammatical tags (in corpora that have undergone the POS tagging described in chapter two) and other analytical tags inserted manually or automatically. Wordlists can be generated to account for individual items or for recurrent sequences of two or more items. This technique will be discussed further below.

Lemmatized frequency lists group together words from the same lemma, i.e. all grammatical inflections of a word. For example, the words *say, said, saying, says* are all part of the lemma SAY. Lemmatization can be done manually using an alphabetical frequency list, or in an automated way which is often based to some degree on lists of predefined lemmas. Different forms of the same lemma tend to vary significantly in terms of their overall frequency, with one particular form tending to be a lot more frequent than others in the lemma. Previous research has also shown that there often are variations in meaning between different variants of the lemma (Stubbs 1996, Tognini-Bonelli 2001). Lemmatized lists also have a place in English language teaching where it can be beneficial to teach all forms of one lemma together and to give priority to the most frequently used form.

The kind of basic information that can be gathered from a frequency list can be illustrated with reference to table 3.1, which shows the 10 most frequent items in the spoken *CANCODE* corpus and in the written component of the *British National Corpus*.[1]

A comparison of the ten most frequent words in the spoken and written corpus highlights some of the key differences between the two discourse modes. Both contain mainly grammatical items, which is expected in terms of the general distribution of different items in the English language. However, the spoken corpus includes the personal pronouns *I* and *You* which shows the interactive nature of the discourse that makes up this corpus. In addition, the item *Yeah* occurs amongst the most frequent items in the spoken data reflecting the pervasive occurrence of listener response tokens in conversation. These three items are at the heart of spoken interaction and the frequency list helps to identify those defining items.

When using frequency lists it is important to be aware of differences in spelling of the same item and the effect of contractions on the frequency count. For example, 'do not' might be contracted as 'don't' in some instances in your corpus, which means that both representations need to be explored before any judgements on their frequency can be made. Furthermore, a frequency list is generated by counting the number of instances of a particular form and is not able to distinguish between different meanings of the same form. This can be a problem when it comes to the analysis of homographs, i.e. words that have the same spelling but different meanings.

Table 3.1 Ten most frequent items in the BNC (written) and CANCODE (spoken).

Frequency rank	BNC (written)	CANCODE (spoken)
1	The	The
2	Of	I
3	And	And
4	A	You
5	In	It
6	To	To
7	Is	A
8	Was	Yeah
9	It	That
10	For	Of

Recurrent continuous sequences

As pointed out above, frequency lists can be generated for recurrent strings of sequences, as well as for individual items.[2] The term recurrent continuous sequences describes the consistency of the data string, however, there are a number of other terms in use to refer to such sequences. Biber *et al.* (1999) use the term 'lexical bundles' while Scott (1996) refers to them as 'clusters'.

Corpus research has highlighted the fact that a large proportion of language is phrasal in nature, that is, that there is an observable tendency for particular items to co-occur in a non-random fashion (see, for example, Sinclair 1996). The attraction between two words is often referred to as collocation and will be discussed in more detail in chapter four. However, the phrasal nature of the English language extends beyond the attraction between two single items and leads to the formation of longer units, which will also be discussed further in chapter four. In terms of frequency lists, an analysis of recurrent sequences can provide a starting point when it comes to the identification of high frequency continuous multi-word units.

The overall length of the sequence has to be determined at the outset. Various software packages can generate such lists and the following lists have been generated with the use of *Wordsmith Tools*. Table 3.2 shows the ten most frequent two-word, three-word and four-word recurrent sequences in the *CANCODE* corpus.

Most of the sequences in this sample, which is taken from a spoken corpus, are concerned with the management of discourse in one way or another. The deictic pointers of the discourse, which specify how something is relative to the speaker or their situation, expressed here through the use of the personal pronouns *you* and *I*, and the sequences associated with them, clearly mark the genre of casual conversation. They are also characteristic of the interactive nature of this type of discourse in which we are constantly seeking to establish mutual understanding, which is expressed through the use of multi-word units such as *know what I mean, I know, I think, do you think,* etc. in table 3.2.

Table 3.2 Ten most frequent two-word, three-word and four-word clusters in CANCODE.

Frequency rank	2-word units		3-word units		4-word units	
1	you know	27,981	I don't know	5,275	you know what I	680
2	I mean	17,105	a lot of	2,856	know what I mean	674
3	I think	13,761	I mean I	2,186	innit isn't it	567
4	in the	13,746	I don't think	2,142	I don't know what	511
5	it was	12,600	do you think	1,504	the end of the	510
6	I don't	11,887	do you want	1,417	at the end of	507
7	of the	10,902	one of the	1,316	do you want to	478
8	and I	9,648	you have to	1,298	a bit of a	457
9	sort of	9,549	it was a	1,273	d'you do you	413
10	do you	9,125	you know I	1,231	do you know what	393

However, while lists of recurrent sequences can be useful in defining different types of language varieties, there are a number of problems with such lists. First of all, when looking at table 3.2 it becomes clear that some sequences are parts of other sequences, and the overall frequency figures have to be assessed in the light of this observation. In the category of four-word sequences, for example, *the end of the* and *at the end of* are likely to both be part of an extended sequence such as *at the end of the day*. In addition, many of these sequences do not appear to have the psycholinguistic quality of phrases in the sense that they are not retrieved from memory as single lexical units. Sequences such as *a bit of a* are only part of a unit, which is possibly completed by a restricted class of nouns (see chapter four for a discussion of the unit a *bit of a* + *X*). The analysis of recurrent sequences in terms of their status as multi-word units thus requires further manual editing and analysis of the frequency output.

Another problem with approaches that are mainly based on frequency information is that those multi-word units that occur with low frequency cannot be captured. This includes many idioms and formulae. Current research in the area of computational corpus linguistics has introduced new techniques for extracting meaningful units from corpora, both on the basis of frequency information (Danielsson 2003) and on the basis of POS tagged corpora which include further annotation of semantic fields (Rayson 2003).

Comparing frequencies in text collections of different sizes

Comparisons of frequency lists from different varieties or domains of English can give an overall picture of distribution in the different corpora and some indication of the orientation of the texts they contain. However, when the texts or text collections are different in overall size, it can be difficult to compare the figures. If we want to compare the frequencies of individual items in two corpora of different sizes, then we can either represent them as a percentage of the overall number of words in the respective corpora or use a norming technique of frequency counts. For this purpose, we divide the raw frequency of individual items by the total number of words in a text. We then need to decide on an appropriate number of words, which forms the basis of the norm, and multiply our results by this figure. The basis of the norm should reflect the overall size of the texts that are being studied. Thus, if the texts or text collections are around 1000 words in length then this should be used as the basis for the norm. This procedure provides a better basis for comparisons of frequencies of individual items in two texts of varying size. It should be pointed out that this procedure is likely to distort the results for very low frequency items.

While norming techniques can facilitate the comparison of individual items across two corpora in terms of overall frequency of occurrence, there are particular calculations that allow us to assess the statistical significance of different frequencies in two corpora.

Keywords

Mike Scott uses the term 'keywords' to refer to those items that occur either with a significantly higher frequency (positive keywords) or with a significantly lower frequency (negative keywords) in a text or collection of texts, when this is compared to a larger reference corpus (Scott 1997). Keywords are identified on the basis of statistical comparisons of word frequency lists derived from the target corpus and the reference corpus. Each item in the target corpus is compared to its equivalent in the reference corpus and its statistical significance of difference calculated via a chi-square test or a log-likelihood analysis (Dunning 1993).[3] Both of these statistics compare actual observed frequencies between two items with their expected frequencies, according to an assumed random distribution.[4] If the difference between observed and expected frequency is large then it is likely that the relationship between the two items is not random, but that other factors influence their relationship. In this way, the procedure generates words that are characteristic, as well as those that are uncharacteristic in a given target corpus. The choice of the reference corpus used as the basis for such a comparison is crucial in this context, as it will affect the output of keywords. For example, in a comparison of a transcript of medical consultations with a reference corpus that consists solely of written texts the characteristics of spoken versus written language may interfere with the analysis of keywords in the medical consultation genre. In the following sample analysis, a small corpus of medical consultations is compared to a larger corpus of general spoken discourse.

Single keywords

Using the log-likelihood function in *Wordsmith Tools*, a keyword analysis was carried out on the basis of a 35,000 word corpus, consisting of the spoken language of health professionals, and the five million word *CANCODE* corpus of general spoken English. The data from the medical consultations was recorded as part of a study of telephone calls made to the British advice helpline provided by the National Health Service, also known as NHS-Direct (see Adolphs *et al.* 2004). The fact that *CANCODE* consists of face-to-face interactions makes the comparison less consistent in terms of the discourse mode, which has to be taken into account in the interpretation of the output. In order to compare the difference between a simple frequency list and a keyword comparison, both types of outputs are shown in tables 3.3 to 3.6.

The raw frequency lists of the two corpora above again show that the most frequent items in both corpora are mainly grammatical ones. The order of frequency in which they occur is slightly different between the two corpora, which is particularly obvious when we consider the distribution of personal pronouns. In the health professional corpus, which is 'other-oriented', the item *you* is the most frequent item, while the same pronoun only ranks as the fourth most frequent item

Table 3.3 Ten most frequent items in the health professional corpus and the CANCODE corpus.

Health professionals (HP)		CANCODE	
You	1,330	The	156,229
The	909	I	142,241
And	762	And	131,869
To	711	You	128,416
It	565	It	99,163
I	481	To	98,309
Of	467	A	86,116
A	466	Yeah	85,497
Right	433	That	78,226
Is	432	Of	72,086

in the corpus of general spoken English. The reverse frequency order of *you* and *I* is maybe the most striking feature in this comparison. In addition, the use of *right* in the health professional corpus versus the use of *yeah* in the corpus of general English shows the overall orientation of the target corpus. Both of these items are listener response tokens, but *right* signals a more transactional nature of the discourse and is often used as an information receipt token, while *yeah* is more informal and used to encourage the speaker to continue with their turn.

While the comparison of frequency lists can help in the characterization of different spoken genres, the keyword analysis below, which is based on a log-likelihood calculation, is better suited to highlight the main elements that are characteristic for a particular text or collection of texts. Table 3.4 shows the top 10 positive keywords (where percentages are not given in the *CANCODE* corpus they are too small to be of interest in this comparison).

This list of keywords gives a better idea of the content of the texts in the HP corpus. References to medication (*antibiotics*), ailments (*diarrhoea*), the nature of

Table 3.4 List of top 10 positive keywords in the health professional corpus compared with CANCODE.

Word	Frequency in health professional corpus	Percentage of HP corpus	Frequency in CANCODE corpus	Percentage of CANCODE corpus	Keyness
OK	120	0.39	227		788.3
Okay	334	1.09	9,615	0.19	622.8
Your	407	1.33	14,768	0.29	609.7
Antibiotics	57	0.19	44		447.8
Diarrhoea	48	0.16	16		421.3
Call	116	0.38	1,326	0.03	400.5
Direct	67	0.22	223		377.5
NHS	34	0.11	2		333.9
Information	86	0.28	802	0.02	328.1
You	1330	4.35	131,865	2.55	327.1

the discourse (*information*), the mode of the discourse (*call*) and the medical context (NHS, Direct) all contribute to the characterization of this corpus. At the same time, the keywords that mark listener responses in an advice-giving setting (*ok, okay*) are marked in this search, as are the pronouns *you* and *your*, which indicate the patient oriented nature of the discourse.

As outlined above, there is a difference between positive and negative keywords. The list in table 3.5 shows the most significant *negative keywords* in the HP corpus, i.e. those words that occur with a significantly lower frequency in the target corpus compared with the reference corpus.

Table 3.5 confirms the results of the analysis of positive keywords. The discourse in the HP corpus is oriented towards the hearer who phones in with a health problem, and we would therefore expect a significant use of the pronouns *you* and *your*. Third person pronouns, on the other hand, imply that the discourse is essentially about somebody other than the speaker or hearer, and the list of negative keywords shows that such items are used with a significantly lower frequency in the HP corpus. The past tense verb *was* is the most significant negative keyword, which confirms the tendency, in the HP corpus, to report current medical concerns in the present tense. While there are some tags in the HP corpus that indicate laughter ([laughs]), there are significantly more of these tags in the corpus of general spoken English, which again is an expected result when we consider the relatively serious nature of medical consultations.

Keyword analyses can be useful in many contexts where the aim relates to the characterization of a particular text or collection of texts. This includes the comparison of different varieties of English, of different discourse modes, such as

Table 3.5 List of top 10 negative keywords in the health professional corpus compared with CANCODE.

Word	Frequency in health professional corpus	Percentage of HP corpus	Frequency in CANCODE corpus	Percentage of CANCODE corpus	Keyness
Was	38	0.12	49,407	0.96	354.4
Mm	21	0.07	41,624	0.8	347.6
I	481	1.57	167,377	3.24	331
She	9	0.03	21,107	0.41	184.2
My	29	0.09	24,435	0.47	137.9
Oh	60	0.2	33,585	0.65	133.8
[LAUGHS]	61	0.2	33,173	0.64	128
He	66	0.22	30,637	0.59	97.2
Her	3		10,086	0.2	95.2
Were	13	0.04	12,593	0.24	77.4
Said	14	0.05	12,322	0.24	71.4
They	113	0.37	37,974	0.73	68.1
Think	57	0.19	23,702	0.46	63.8

spoken versus written, and of writing styles of a particular author. Keywords can also contribute towards an analysis of the general orientation of a text via a further analysis of the keywords that are being generated. In the analysis above, these include mainly medical terms, which are neutral in terms of their connotations. However, comparing the style of individual writers or of particular newspapers through a keyword analysis may reveal instances of more 'loaded' language and content that characterizes the target texts. A subsequent analysis of concordance lines of individual keywords can be used to further explore this type of orientation.

Key sequences

The analysis of keywords can be extended to include extended recurrent sequences. In table 3.6 a key sequences comparison was carried out on the basis of the Health Professional corpus introduced above and the five million word *CANCODE* corpus as a reference corpus.

The calculation of key sequences provides us with even stronger evidence of the particular domain in which the HP discourse has been collected. As could be expected, quite a few of the recurrent sequences in table 3.6 form part of the automated responses that mark the beginning of the telephone interaction with NHS Direct. Other sequences relate to the gathering of basic information about the caller. It is interesting to note that the most significant negative key sequence, i.e. the one that occurs with a significantly lower frequency in the HP corpus, in comparison to the corpus of casual conversation, is *I don't know*. Again, this is not surprising and highlights the professional nature of this encounter where the emphasis is on providing knowledge and advice.

Table 3.6 also shows one of the potential problems with the way in which data is represented when it comes to the analysis of recurrent sequences. The software identifies individual words in terms of spaces between characters. This means that N H S is counted as three individual words, which obviously affects the calculation

Table 3.6 Ten most significant positive key sequences in the health professional corpus.

Sequence	Frequency in HP corpus	Frequency in CANCODE	Keyness
NH S Direct	46	0	465.8
N H S	58	203	313.3
Just bear with	26	6	232.4
Call you back	26	8	226.2
Bear with me	28	20	218.5
Date of birth	28	23	213.6
Your date of	25	11	208.9
You're calling from	15	0	151.9
Manage their services	13	0	131.6
However anybody with	13	0	131.6

of the recurrent sequence. To avoid this type of problem we can either replace the acronym in the target corpus by a continuous sequence without spaces, or correct the calculation at the output stage.

Other statistical measures

There are a number of other statistical analyses that are based on frequency information and that can be used to distinguish different genres, text-types and authors. Multivariate analysis, which is a statistical method that involves investigating the relationship between multiple variables, including factor analysis, correspondence analysis and cluster analysis, can be useful when we want to establish relationships between a number of different linguistic features and their frequency of occurrence across different texts and text types. An introduction to this type of analysis would be beyond the scope of this book, but is further detailed in Biber *et al*. (1998).

Summary

This chapter has introduced a number of basic techniques in electronic text analysis including:

- **The calculation of basic information about a text or collection of texts**. This is an option in a number of concordance packages and includes sentence length, word length, number of paragraphs, ratio between the number of running words in a text and the number of different words in a text (type-token ratio). This information can be used to establish an initial picture of the consistency of text(s).
- **Word lists**. These can be generated in different rank orders including alphabetical, frequency, according to part of speech (POS) and lemma. Wordlists can be used to inform research questions about a text or text collection and to compare two sets of texts or text collections.
- **Keywords and key sequences**. These are words and sequences that occur with a frequency that is significantly higher or significantly lower in a target corpus when it is compared to a larger reference corpus. Keywords and key sequences can be used to profile individual texts and to provide evidence as to the overall orientation of a text.

This chapter has focused mainly on the role of frequency information in relation to the characterization of whole texts or collections of texts. However, as already mentioned, frequency lists can be a good starting point for concordance searches and can act as a hypothesis-forming procedure. Further concordance searches of frequently used items can be helpful in determining patterns of usage with reference to other linguistic variables or text domains. The same applies for any other word that has not been generated through a frequency list but that is of interest for another reason. The next chapter will deal with the exploration of the concordance output.

Activities

1. Using any of the software programs described in this chapter, create a frequency list of the resource you have assembled in chapter two. What do the frequency counts tell you about your resource? Compare this frequency list with that of another corpus, such as *British National Corpus* for example. What are the main differences and how do they relate to the particular genre of your texts.

2. The following three words are amongst the 50 most frequent types in the *CANCODE* spoken corpus: *know, think, just*. Use any of the online spoken corpora referred to on the book companion website and carry out an analysis of their discourse functions. Do the results of your analysis explain why these items might be more frequent in spoken than in written discourse? Now repeat this exercise with a written corpus and analyse differences in distribution following the procedures outlined in this chapter.

Further reading

In the area of corpus linguistics, as well as in the broader area of electronic text analysis, quantitative elements tend to be a staple part of most types of analysis. As such we find that a frequency analysis accompanies most studies discussed in this volume and it might therefore be sensible to carry out further reading in relation to particular research themes or questions that are of interest to the individual reader.

In terms of publications that are specifically concerned with the issue of frequency, Leech *et al.* (2001) provide a comprehensive guide to frequency analysis and data in the *British National Corpus*. Various types of statistical analysis for language data are discussed in Oakes (1998) and a critical discussion of quantitative methods in corpus linguistics is covered by Stubbs (1995).

Notes

1. The frequency list of the written component of the British National Corpus has been adapted from the frequency list on the companion website to Leech *et al.* (2001) at <http://www.comp.lancs.ac.uk/ucrel/bncfreq/>. The frequencies of *to* which are presented on this website as two entries reflecting the different grammatical roles have been added up and presented as a single entry in the list used here.

2. See, for example, Biber *et al.* (1999) who use the extraction of recurrent continues sequences as the basis for a discussion of lexical bundles.

3. For further information on the log-likelihood calculation and an interactive log-likelihood calculator see <http://ucrel.lancs.ac.uk/llwizard.html>. An integrated web-based corpus processing interface developed by Rayson (2005) can be accessed at <http://www.comp.lancs.ac.uk/ucrel/wmatrix/>.

4. One of the problems with the chi-square calculation is that it can produce distorted statistics if the expected frequencies of individual items are low, particularly when words in a small corpus are compared with a large reference corpus. It is therefore not advisable to use the chi-square calculation under those circumstances.

4 Exploring words and phrases in use: basic techniques

Introduction

Following on from the analysis of frequencies in different texts and text collections introduced in the last chapter, this chapter will deal with the analysis of individual words and phrases at the concordance level. As such, it moves from the characterization of texts and text-types to the description of individual items. As already mentioned in the previous chapter, frequency lists can be a good starting point for concordance searches and can be used to generate hypotheses about the relationship between particular linguistic choices and different domains of discourse. Individual words or phrases might be chosen on the basis of their significance to a particular research question. An analysis of how age and ageing is represented in the media, for example, might prompt an analysis of those items that refer to the process of ageing. Concordance analyses can thus again be used both to generate and to test hypotheses, as well as to automate manual processes of counting words and structures.

The electronic analysis of large text collections has led to a new level of language description that is based on the extraction of lexico-grammatical patterns from concordance data. This kind of study has shown that lexis and grammar do not exist independently from one another but rather that they are inextricably linked (Sinclair 1991). The inspection of concordance data can reveal such patterns of co-dependence and has thus had a major impact on the way in which we describe language in use. However, apart from lexico-grammatical patterns, the study of concordance data has also highlighted the possibility of describing other properties of individual words and phrases in a systematic manner. In particular, the description of the overall connotations of a word with reference to the immediate co-text has become possible through systematic analysis of concordance outputs. While the immediate application of these advances has been most noticeable in the area of lexicography, it is not restricted to this area and has had a considerable impact on other areas concerned with the study of discourse, including, amongst others, critical discourse analysis, forensic linguistics, English language teaching and sociolinguistics.

This chapter provides an introduction to the analysis of individual words and phrases through the study of concordance output. It starts by outlining some of the basic ways in which concordance data can be presented and then moves on to an introduction to the various aspects of meaning that become observable through concordance data.

The concordance output

A concordance programme arranges all instances of a particular search item in a way that makes the search item appear in the centre of the page. The search item is also often referred to as the 'node' and the items to the left and to the right of the node are called the 'span'. The length of the span can be specified in most programmes but, for descriptive purposes, a span of four or five items to the left and to the right of the node is a commonly used range. In the descriptions of concordance data, the node is often represented by N and the items to the left and to the right as N-1, N-2, etc. and N+1, N+2, etc., respectively. There is some flexibility in most programmes as to what can be specified as a search item, including single words, phrases and grammatical tags. In addition, it is usually possible to define wildcards to introduce a certain level of flexibility into the search.

A simple example of a Key Word in Context (KWIC) concordance is shown below. One particular area of interest in the analysis of spoken discourse is how people do things with words (Austin 1962). That is, how do we encode particular functions in social interactions? While most utterances contribute to the performance of language functions, there are a number of verbs that are particularly explicit in naming such functions. These are often called speech act verbs or performative verbs. An analysis of corpus data can illustrate the extent to which such verbs are used in a direct or modalized manner. Below is an example of a concordance output of the verb *disagree* from the five million word spoken *CANCODE*. Since one of the main aims in casual conversation is to maintain and, where possible, increase levels of convergence between speakers, we would not expect to find many instances of this verb in a corpus of casual conversation:

Yeah. Well I	**disagree**	with that because you get more people
got from A to B. And therefore if you can't	**disagree**	with them all you can do is agree with
aspects. I mean why aren't we if like I	**disagree**	with that this great great
up new. But cos the Chinese never	**disagree**	openly. Yeah. They er
different expressions. Now you might	**disagree**	with them but you're supposed to be a
Do you	**disagree**	with caffeine in
now you've got most agree and most	**disagree**	Yeah. Yeah.
you know the great literary critics you can't	**disagree**	with them. They they kick the dust over

The green one? I beg to	**disagree**	I beg to differ.
I'm glad you said that cos I totally	**disagree**	with the view that you it's right

The overall number of instances of this item in CANCODE is 44, of which the above is a sample of 10 concordance lines, arranged in a KWIC layout. A sample has been chosen here because of space limitations. However, where possible it is useful to examine the entire concordance output, only using randomization procedures for highly frequent words where it is necessary to make the output more manageable.

In order to facilitate the analysis of concordance outputs further, most software packages allow an alphabetical sort to the left or to the right of the search word. The output below is sorted alphabetically one word to the left:

you know the great literary critics you *can't*	**disagree**	with them. They they kick the dust
got from A to B. And therefore if you *can't*	**disagree**	with them all you can do is agree with
aspects. I mean why aren't we if like *I*	**disagree**	with that this great great
Yeah. Well *I*	**disagree**	with that because you get more people
different expressions. Now you *might*	**disagree**	with them but you're supposed to be a
now you've got most agree and *most*	**disagree**	Yeah. Yeah.
up new. But cos the Chinese *never*	**disagree**	openly. Yeah. They er
The green one? I beg *to*	**disagree**	I beg to differ.
I'm glad you said that cos I *totally*	**disagree**	with the view that you it's right
Do *you*	**disagree**	with caffeine in

This alphabetical search shows that *I* is only the subject in four of the instances (twice in N-1 position and twice in other position in the left span). One of these is a phrase (I beg to disagree). The output thus shows that, in the majority of instances, the verb *disagree* is not used by speakers to express their disagreement with one another. In fact, when we consider the patterns to the right of the node, we see that in the majority of instances the speaker does not disagree with the hearer directly but with others who are not involved in the conversation or with their views.

Apart from the KWIC concordance output, there are other ways in which concordance data can be represented, which can be useful if longer stretches of co-text are required. Most software packages allow you to specify the size of the span and/or allow a KWIC output for individual instances to be extended to a larger discourse stretch. An example of a concordance output from the British National corpus of the word *disagree*, that is based on the sentence as a unit, is shown below.[1] The letters and numbers at the start of the concordance lines identify the source of the individual text extracts in the BNC:

A68 1653 The commission moved away from the idea that Christians agree on what is important and **disagree** only on what is trivial.

A6J 1749 And although she seems to **disagree** with its overall drift, she tells me she's in complete accord with my views on what she called my ';blasted reconstruction';.';

AC4 2757 Bella opened her mouth to **disagree**, glanced at Harriet Shakespeare and shut it again.

ADW 294 The style of discussion –; Zuwaya rhetoric –; was generally subdued and relaxed, governed by two apparent rules: first, it was shameful to display personal interests openly; and, secondly, it was impolite to **disagree** with guests or hosts.

AN4 873 Yet in view of the problems discussed in the first section of this chapter, it will be necessary to **disagree** with a number of Landry's principal arguments.

AN8 1345 It was a considerable risk; he knew perfectly well that Graham Moloney would certainly **disagree** with him with some violence.

AR8 471 Both DuVivier and Byrne wrote accounts of the raid fairly soon afterwards, and although they **disagree** on details, the main story is clear.

ART 537 Morrissey makes a lousy rock critic though it is hard to **disagree** with his put-downs.

ART 828 The Smiths have never really conformed to the pop ideal, being larger than life but twice as monotonous, although some would **disagree**.

While this kind of display can be useful if we want to analyse the complete sentence in which the search word occurs, it can be difficult to observe any patterns that surround the search item. The KWIC concordance is thus better suited when it comes to analysing patterns of use.

A KWIC concordance can be generated either by using a word or a phrase, as well as with the use of wildcards as in the following example of the node say* which shows different continuations of *say* in the CANCODE corpus:

and I went around like that now	**saying**	What's your name and What
listening cos you were downstairs? Ah I was	**saying**	about that. It's a good service actually
him I expect. What a nasty thing to	**say**	laughs I think have we got here. Are
I didn't understand what what they were	**saying**	never mind the poor French people
were going to do it but there we are. But she's	**saying**	that em loads of people that they're me
You know what they	**say**	the old saying the more writing you do the
I never know what to put when it	**says**	home address. Em yeah it's your permant

The use of wildcards allows us to generate all forms that include a specified sequence of letters. This can be useful if we want to include different parts of a particular lemma (but note that this search does not include the past tense *said*).

A further way of manipulating the search criteria is by providing a second word that occurs in the context of the search word within a specified span to its left or right. In a concordance of Shakespeare's plays, for example, we may want to study the frequency or the patterns of those instances where the word *love* occurs in the context of *hate*, or where it occurs in the context of the name of a particular character. Adding a context word to a concordance search allows us to study patterns that are not restricted to a continuous sequence. The following is an example of a concordance output of the word *politics* with the specified context word *British*:[2]

GT9 364 attack on the incestuous nature of *British*	**politics**.	Chesterton became editor
CBB 703 anti-Semitic figure in *British* Fascist	**politics**	during the 1930s, and his
F9M 1466 Politics of Today De Black *British*	**Politics**	of Dis Day. The Old
F9M 1462 gu awey De Black *British*	**Politics**	of Today, Many Poets

This type of search allows us to narrow down the output without having to specify adjacent items. Again, we can make use of wildcards to include different parts of speech of the search word in the output as shown in the concordance below. This concordance is based on the same corpus and concordance software as the one above but has been further specified to include items that begin with the form *politic**:

A87 274 of the *British* role and lack of clear	**political**	direction – a far cry from the
A87 265 a rare display of harmony the *British*	**political**	Establishment last night united
JXL 123 support of the *British* Residency, making	**political**	life a triangular struggle that did
A87 259 centred Europe. But what do *British*	**politicians**	want to see? It's sadly typical of the
A87 267 at *British* isolation from events. Among	**politicians**	who have spent their lives working
F9M 1466 Black Politics of Today De Black *British*	**Politics**	of Dis Day. The Old Truth Rumour

This type of concordance can be useful when the research aim is to identify particular themes of usage rather than the lexico-grammatical patterns of individual word forms.

When the overall aim is to analyse grammatical forms or constructions, a tagged corpus can be used to search specifically for such tags. The following is a small sample of concordance lines that have been generated on the basis of a search for *I * [VFpres]* to show instances where *I* is followed by a present tense verb in the *CANCODE* corpus (note that other tags have been deleted):

actually so can I can	**[VFpres]**	I
I and I I believe	**[VFpres]**	we
I know	**[VFpres]**	I wish I wish I
Yeah I think	**[VFpres]**	it
Yeah. I think I think	**[VFpres]**	I

It is of course also possible to use a tagged corpus to identify all instances of a specific part of speech which is not part of a particular structure such as in the output above.

Describing words and phrases in use

As discussed above, the study of concordance outputs provides overwhelming evidence for patterning in language and thus makes descriptions that are based on isolated lexical items outside of their context of use questionable. Sinclair (1996) argues therefore that a new unit of meaning should be explored that extends beyond the single word and takes into account in its description the properties and patterns that are revealed by concordance analysis. In order to describe the nature of individual units of meaning, Sinclair (ibid) suggests four parameters: collocation, colligation, semantic preference and semantic prosody. Collocation refers to the habitual co-occurrence of words and will be discussed in more detail below. Drawing on Firth (1957), Sinclair uses the term colligation to refer to the co-occurrence of grammatical choices. The semantic preference of a lexical item or expression is the semantic grouping of the words that co-occur on either side of the node. In his discussion of the expression *the naked eye*, Sinclair (1996) finds that many of the verbs and adjectives preceding this expression are related to the concept of 'vision'. The verbs 'see' and 'seen' together occur 25 times within four words to the left of the expression in a sample of 151 examples of *the naked eye*. Sinclair (ibid) introduces, as his fourth parameter in the description of the unit of meaning, the concept of 'semantic prosody'. Semantic prosodies are connotations that arise from the co-text of a lexical items and are not easily detected with reference to intuition (Louw 1993). Semantic prosodies have mainly been described in terms of their positive or negative polarity (Sinclair 1991, Stubbs 1995) but also in terms of their association with 'tentativeness/indirectness/face saving' (McCarthy 1998: 22). These four parameters can be used as the basis for a description of words and phrases in a concordance output.

The following output shows a random number of 38 lines of the sequence *a bit of a*, which was identified as one of the most frequent four-word sequences in the *CANCODE* corpus in the last chapter.[3]

area) and back to the fridge again. Sounds	**a bit of a**	performance, but it's actually the way we
If you want to give your golf partner	**a bit of a**	surprise, drive off with one of these new
she told us we had to leave. [p] Not that's	**a bit of a**	long story, but I'm sure you could
22, MIDFIELDER/DEFENDER [/h]	**A bit of a**	later corner from Bath who was a second
him slipping off the rails and becoming	**a bit of a**	delinquent; after a troubled educational
returning to the Puerto Rican capital can be	**a bit of a**	jolt, but there are still ample
fine says the Arsenal right-back It's still	**a bit of a**	mystery as to what the problem was, but I'
up to be a fine man, most of the time. He's	**a bit of a**	scrapper, though." [p] Autumn knew it had
moments to me. Just time enough to have	**a bit of a**	chat with her." Indeed?" [name] rolled his
her faulty syntax and the fact that she was	**a bit of a**	monster to her family, she has probably
training," he says yes I did feel that I had	**a bit of a**	knack for it [p] His rise, which seemed
the things which make the hero emerge as	**a bit of a**	git. [p] The plot concerns an imperfect
and growing companies suffering from	**a bit of a**	hangover after the Easter break and the

	a bit of a	
uring adjournments. [p] However, I'm	**a bit of a**	news fiend myself and just took a radio
five in the first seven games [p] I've hit	**a bit of a**	barren patch since then, so I wouldn't
hicker Plot. [p] The band have always been	**a bit of a**	pop oddity but constant touring and an
after a shopping trip. [p] And it looked	**a bit of a**	squeeze as mum manoeuvred out of their
Now he was	**a bit of a**	lost soul who spent his time painting
from his own party, and so I think there's	**a bit of a**	new tradition that he's seeking to
Oh that's nice. [F06] But you know I had	**a bit of a**	fight to get it [M01] [000] Yeah. [F06]
[M01] Mm. [M03] What's she trying to get	**a bit of a**	cheque book journalism that's what it
all these offers for [name] I think it's just	**a bit of a**	booster for them to be honest. [M01] Mm.
[tc text=tuts] No cigarettes. [ZGY]	**a bit of a**	nightmare really. [F0X] Becoming a bit of
So I had to leave it [tc text=pause] which is	**a bit of a**	shame. It's a shame I didn't get the
ldn't it. [M02] Yes. Nothing special I was	**a bit of a**	problem to the teachers but er I've got a
ZF1] it was [ZF0] it was [F01] Oh were you	**a bit of a**	gimmick? [F02] a good time to go
[M01] Okay [M09] Erm and we s we had	**a bit of a**	discussion about this at work and
company name [ZZ0] was certainly taking	**a bit of a**	nosedive four or five years ago. [M02]
Mm. [M02] So I suppose there there's been	**a bit of a**	sort of erm a trade-off. The other thing
upport [ZGY] [F01] Mm. [M01] So we had	**a bit of a**	gun to our head and so [F01] Mm. [M01] it
[ZF1] you can [ZF0] you can build up	**a bit of a**	bond with them and that in that short
oscillation has been active er So it's still	**a bit of a**	puzzle. [M01] So it might just be that
well as well. She's got [F06] So she was in	**a bit of a**	mood and everyone kept taking the mick
Yeah [M01] you quickly. You said there was	**a bit of a**	difference of opinion about what should
Yeah [F02] If you read between the lines it's	**a bit of a**	farce [tc text=laughs] [M01] You know the
kept going took on [name] in turn they got in	**a bit of a**	mess the United defence it rolled across
speak to him about. [ZF1] It's [ZF0] it's all	**a bit of a**	nightmare [ZGY] [F01] [tc text=laughs]
[F01] Erm right. [tc text=sighs] We made	**a bit of a**	mistake. We both went to see a

The issue of collocation will be dealt with separately below so we will here focus on the other parameters, i.e. colligation, semantic preference and semantic prosody. In the majority of instances, the colligation structure of the sequence *a bit of a* is as follows: (to be/to have) a+bit+of+a+(adjective)+noun. From this concordance output, we can see that this phrase carries a negative semantic prosody, which becomes obvious in the choices to the right of the search phrase that it modifies. The overall concordance output shows a tendency for semantic preferences to include people, events and states of mind. In particular references are made to people who are here associated with a negative meaning such as *monster, pop oddity, scrapper, delinquent* and *lost soul*. The output also includes evaluative references to particular situations and states of mind that carry a negative meaning in the respective instances such as *mistake, nightmare, farce, puzzle, problem, shame, hangover, mystery* and *performance*. Other items that carry a direct negative semantic prosody or are used in an overall negative context, complete the rest of the instances of this concordance. Semantic prosodies will be explored further in subsequent chapters, particularly in relation to the study of language and ideology in chapter six.

The concordance output of *a bit of a* leads us into the next section of the description of multi-word units. The restrictions placed on the items that follow this sequence, in terms of their semantic prosody and their semantic preference, define the scope of the variation to the right of the sequence. The result of the co-occurrence with a particular set of items is the formation of phraseology and multi-word units, which will be discussed in more detail in the next section.

Multi-word units and collocation

In the previous chapter we have looked at the way in which frequencies can be generated not only for individual lexical items but also for recurrent sequences or clusters of words. Some of those recurrent sequences may be considered to be meaningful multi-word units, i.e. sequences that are mentally processed as a single unit. Other units that are generated through frequency information might simply reflect the nature of the individual data-sets on which they are based. Thus the recurrent sequence *the the the* which occurs in the spoken CANCODE corpus mainly shows the type of disfluency we would expect from a corpus which consists mainly of casual conversation.

Sinclair (1996) argues that there are two principles on which language is based, the 'idiom principle' and the 'open choice principle'. The 'idiom principle' operates when speakers make use of lexicalized and semi-lexicalized phrases, which are stored whole in long term memory and retrieved as single items. This principle is opposed to the 'open choice principle', according to which language is based on grammatical rules and is selected 'slot by slot'. Corpus investigations have shown that a large proportion of discourse is organized according to more or less rigid associations between individual words (see Schmitt and Carter 2004 for an overview), as in the concordance analysis of the structure *a bit of a* + X described above.

The term *multi-word units* is used here as an umbrella term for sequences of interrelated words which are retrieved from memory as single lexical units. They occur with varying degrees of fixedness and include formulae (e.g. *have a nice day*), metaphors (e.g. *kick the bucket*) and collocations (e.g. *rancid butter*) (see Moon 1998 and Wray 2002 for an overview). The description and conceptualization of multi-word units are a key concern in many different areas of language study ranging from psycholinguistics to Natural Language Processing (NLP). Each discipline has preferred ways of identifying multi-word units. These include intuitive identification, the use of discourse analytical techniques and automatic extraction from electronic texts. The classification into different types of multi-word units tends to be linked to particular characteristics. Formulae, for example, are marked by their pragmatic function while collocations are marked by their frequency of co-occurrence in discourse. Multi-word units are closely linked to the particular genre in which they occur (see for example Oakey 2002 and Simpson 2004 for discussions of multi-word units in academic writing). Carter (1988: 163) defines collocation as, 'an aspect of lexical cohesion, which embraces a "relationship" between lexical items that regularly co-occur'. This relationship can be general or text specific, as well as genre specific. There are various ways in which the attraction between individual lexical items, or in fact between multi-word units and lexical items can be determined. The two techniques that will be briefly discussed here are:

- Inspection of concordance data either without further automated analysis or with the help of frequency information.
- Mutual information.

There are many instances where the close observation of the concordance output can be enough to highlight patterns of co-occurrence. Stubbs (1995, 1996) and Sinclair (1991) study lexical items that collocate with negative events, such as the word *cause* or the phrase *set in*. Concordance searches of such items reveal that most of the nouns immediately following or preceding these verbs are negative, such as *bad weather*, *epidemic*, etc. A search of the word *cause* in the CANCODE corpus reveals similar patterns, with recurrent instances of *cause damage* (6), *cause confusion* (2), *cause drama* (3) and various other combinations that carry a negative connotation. Wordsmith Tools provides a functionality for representing the words in the span that surround the node in terms of their frequency of occurrence (see table 4.1).

One of the problems of a mere frequency calculation of items that occur within the span of a particular search word is that all of the high frequency, mainly grammatical, items automatically occur at the top of the list. However, since we can expect these to be frequent in the environment of any node item, their co-occurrence is not significant. A list such as the one in table 4.1 therefore has to be edited further to exclude high frequency grammatical items. This has been done from the tenth most frequent collocate onwards in table 4.1. The remaining instances are lexicalized items, which can be discussed in terms of their status as candidate collocates. The majority of these items have negative connotations, which is in line with the results of Stubbs' and Sinclair's analyses. The word *people*, however, does not fit into this pattern. When we consider the positions of this item in the span, we see that it occurs in positions that are substantially removed from the node word. Yet, it is an interesting collocate to take into account as an unspecified agent associated with the act of causing negative events.

Mutual information

Apart from deriving collocations through observation of concordance data or through raw frequency information about individual items in the span, there are statistical methods that can be used to account for lexical attraction. Such methods compare the expected frequency with which two words co-occur in a corpus with the actual frequency of co-occurrence. In order to make this calculation, the program calculates the overall frequency of the search word and the individual words of the span in a given corpus. It then calculates the joint frequency of the two, i.e.

Table 4.1 Fifty most frequent items that occur in the span of the word *cause* in CANCODE.

	Word	Total	Fifth word left	Fourth word left	Third word left	Second word left	First word left	Node	First word right	Second word right	Third word right	Fourth word right	Fifth word right
1	CAUSE	250	0	5	1	1	3	233	1	0	5	1	0
2	THE	105	9	6	5	12	23	0	9	8	10	11	12
3	AND	65	7	7	7	4	8	0	7	10	7	4	4
4	THAT	57	11	10	9	6	7	0	3	1	3	1	6
5	THEY	37	4	1	4	7	6	0	0	5	4	2	4
6	YOU	35	0	7	2	1	0	0	2	6	7	4	6
7	CAN	32	2	3	3	3	15	0	0	1	0	2	3
8	YEAH	28	1	2	2	3	1	0	1	6	4	4	4
9	BUT	26	6	4	1	2	0	0	2	1	2	4	4
10	EFFECT	26	7	0	0	1	0	0	11	2	2	3	0
[...]													
40	PROBLEMS	8	0	0	0	0	0	0	6	1	1	0	0
44	DAMAGE	7	0	1	0	0	0	0	2	2	2	0	0
57	CONCERN	5	0	0	0	0	0	0	4	1	0	0	0
65	PEOPLE	5	0	2	1	0	0	0	0	0	0	1	1
69	VIRUSES	5	0	0	0	3	2	0	0	0	0	0	0

how often they co-occur. This is referred to as the raw joint frequency. This type of measure does not tell us much about the strength of lexical attraction, since individual words in the span may occur with a very high frequency, as would be the case with grammatical items. The calculation of mutual information thus compares the observed probability of co-occurrence of two items with the expected probability of their co-occurrence. The latter is based on the assumption of random distribution. The ratio between expected and observed frequency is called *Mutual Information*. The higher this score is, the stronger the attraction between the words. A mutual information analysis of the word *cause* based on the Collins Wordbanks *Online* corpus is shown in table 4.2.

The advantages of using mutual information over simple frequency information, as illustrated above, become clear when we consider this output. The grammatical items, which occupied most of the rows in the previous table, are no longer included in the mutual information output, which makes the analysis of collocates more straightforward. The negative connotations of the collocates are even more apparent in this output. Due to the nature of the MI score calculation

Table 4.2 Mutual information analysis of the word *cause* in the Collins WordbanksOnline corpus.

Collocate	Corpus freq	Joint freq	Significance
celebre	16	16	10.100,54
proximate	16	7	8.907,776
grevious	11	4	8.640,963
abscesses	10	3	8.363,402
sacrospinalis	17	3	7.597,791
grievous	83	14	7.532,6
drowsiness	31	5	7.468,01
championed	91	13	7.292,906
suffocation	21	3	7.292,906
commonest	49	6	7.070,491
isd	35	4	6.970,945
intestinal	46	5	6.898,587
precipitating	29	3	6.827,196
dizziness	70	7	6.778,281
irritations	31	3	6.730,971
creutzfeldt	33	3	6.640,764
deafness	56	5	6.614,766
malfunction	45	4	6.608,339
havoc	171	15	6.589,229
blockage	47	4	6.545,597

we find that the results are slightly distorted in that a high score is achieved by those words that have a low frequency in the corpus (see Stubbs 1995). More recognizable patterns can be found in the combination of items that have a high corpus frequency (e.g. cause havoc, cause blockage, cause dizziness).

There are a number of other methods of extracting collocations from corpora, including t-scores and z-scores, which are explained in more detail in a number of corpus linguistics publications (see for example Barnbrook 1996).

While the calculation of mutual information gives us a better idea of the attraction between two items, it does not provide any evidence of extended patterns of co-occurrence between multiple items. A concordance search of the collocates *cause* + *grevious/grievous* in the output shows that all instances are part of the phrase *cause grievous bodily harm*. A secondary concordance analysis of the collocates can reveal such patterns of multi-word units.

Summary

The applications of concordance analysis are many and varied. Concordance analysis has a key place in language description and lexicography, especially because such an analysis can reveal patterns of co-occurrence and association that not only challenge some traditional beliefs about language as a slot-and-filler system, but also lead to insights that are not easily generated on the basis of intuition alone. However, there are a number of other applications of this type of analysis, which will be explored in more detail in the next four chapters. These include the analysis of semantic prosodies with reference to ideology and point of view, as well as in relation to English language teaching. This chapter has shown how concordance outputs can be presented in different ways and how individual words and phrases can be subjected to further automated and interpretative analysis.

Activities

1. Carry out an analysis of the word *stuff* on the basis of the concordance output taken from the CANCODE corpus. The concordance output has been sorted alphabetically at N-1. Can you identify any patterns in this data that relate to any of the concepts discussed in this chapter, including grammatical integration, collocation, semantic preference and semantic prosody? Does the immediate environment of the individual concordance lines give you any indication as to the type of context in which they are used?

Geometry? Geometry. And	**stuff**	like that. Geometry I don't part
almost in a sense of surprise and	**stuff**	like that.
There's a lot of organization and	**stuff**.	Yeah. God.
just planning all like the work and	**stuff**	to be done on it.
your mind and bought a ticket and	**stuff**.	Well+
in certain areas of Manhattan and	**stuff**.	Yeah. I think that's
down for the funeral and	**stuff**.	It's all a bit of a hassle
He goes to meetings and	**stuff**	so he pops over. Right
it so I can put it up at shows and	**stuff**	
you need all the firelighters and	**stuff**	to go with it so.
us about on these back waters and	**stuff**.	Coconut palms.
like salads and bread buns and	**stuff**	like that and jacket potatoes
She wants to move her	**stuff**.	Stuff. Who?
What? You must not leave	**stuff**	like this under the sofa.
because she shouldn't leave	**stuff**	in her bin anyway if she
We've got so much	**stuff**	there there's no way we're
Because there's so much	**stuff**	crammed into it. And er
don't need that". A whole load of	**stuff**.	Er but other things I said "Oh
I don't like simple	**stuff**.	I'm gonna have a chocolate.
What are we going to do with the	**stuff**.	I mean I bet that's a very
soapy water and we'll wash the	**stuff**	out here. Yeah.
Mm. What's all this	**stuff**?	What about
Come on then. Let's get this	**stuff**	washed. I mean did you not

Further reading

There are a number of comprehensive books available which discuss ways in which we can derive patterns of meaning from concordance output in great detail. These include, for example, Sinclair (2003) and Stubbs (2001). The basic parameters of the unit of meaning discussed in this chapter are outlined in Sinclair (1991,1996), as well as in a collection of key papers published in Sinclair (2004a). Building on some of the concepts developed in corpus-based lexicography, Hoey (2005) introduces the idea of *lexical priming* and illustrates how certain words are primed for use in particular contexts and co-texts.

In addition, any of the introductory publications mentioned in the further reading section of chapter one deal with the analysis of concordance output. And, Hunston (2002) gives an overview of the many different areas of application of concordance analyses.

Notes

1. This concordance has been generated via the *BNC* simple search online facility at <http://sara.natcorp.ox.ac.uk/lookup.html>.
2. This output is based on a sample of the *British National Corpus* using the *Compleat Lexical Tutor* web-interface at <http://www.lextutor.ca/>. The *BNC* source identification codes were added subsequently to the concordance output.
3. This output has been generated via the *Collins WordbanksOnline* English corpus at <http://www.collins.co.uk/Corpus/CorpusSearch.aspx>.

5 The electronic analysis of literary texts

Introduction

As outlined in chapter two, the accessibility of literary corpora and electronic text archives readily available for use via the internet and CD-ROMs is ever increasing. This development affords the exploration of literary texts with the use of quantitative and qualitative methods, including those that have been developed in the area of corpus linguistics.

While there is a rich tradition in the use of statistics in the analysis of literary style, also known as stylometry, the use of corpus linguistic techniques, such as those described in the previous two chapters, is still in its early stages. In the area of stylometry much research has been devoted to the characterization of authorship. Burrows (1987), for example, explores the analysis of frequency profiles of individual words in Jane Austen novels, partly in relationship to specific idiolects of particular characters. Similarly, in a study of a 30,000-word corpus of novels by different authors, Hoover (2002) demonstrates how authorial style can be identified by means of statistical analysis of highly frequent words and word clusters. His study combines the use of statistics with corpus linguistic methods of analysing sequences and clusters of words.

Over the past decade there have been a number of studies that have highlighted the potential of a corpus approach for the interpretation of literary texts (see for example Stubbs 2005). This approach, which is now often referred to as corpus stylistics (Semino and Short 2004), shares some of the criticisms that have been voiced in relation to stylistics in general, particularly with regard to the selective attention to particular features (Fish 1996), and the status of literary interpretations generated on the basis of a purely linguistic analysis (see Stubbs 2005 for a discussion). Yet, there is now a considerable body of research in the area of stylistics that illustrates how the analysis of literary texts using linguistics frameworks can both generate new insights, and provide evidence for established interpretations. The same applies to the area of corpus stylistics, which is currently being used to complement other types of stylistic and literary analysis, as well as an approach in its own right.

This chapter will illustrate how techniques developed in the area of corpus linguistics can be applied to the study of literary texts. The chapter starts out with an overview of different approaches in corpus stylistics, before moving on to the issue of annotating literary corpora to facilitate such approaches. The main part of the chapter is devoted to a sample analysis, which illustrates the use of corpus linguistic techniques in the analysis of point of view in a novel.

Using computers to analyse literary texts: basic techniques

Most corpus stylistics studies are designed to either test or facilitate interpretations of a literary text or collection of texts. Existing interpretations tend to be based on analytical concepts and frameworks that have emerged outside the realm of electronic text analysis, such as the analysis of speech and thought presentation for example, a key framework in the area of literary linguistics which we will return to later. Thus, the things we ask the computer to do, and the way in which we prepare or annotate our electronic text, is often influenced by a previous discussion of a literary text or by an existing approach to it. In a corpus stylistic analysis of Joseph Conrad's *Heart of Darkness*, Stubbs (2005) illustrates how this approach can provide added evidence for themes already identified by literary critics. One of the themes Stubbs considers is that of vagueness and uncertainty, which has been linked to only a limited number of content words in previous interpretations (such as the words *vague* and *indistinct*). He shows that a concordance search of the text for other lexical items that denote vagueness and uncertainty, such as *something* and *some sort*, supports the status of vagueness as a core theme in this text. In the same paper, Stubbs also illustrates how a comparison of frequently used phrases in *Heart of Darkness* with those that occur in the 100-million word *British National Corpus*, reveals further evidence of the theme of vagueness. He analyses the most frequent five-word sequences in the *British National Corpus*, which all include spatial references, such as *at the end of the* and *in the centre of the* (Stubbs 2005: 20). When comparing these with Conrad's place expression, Stubbs notes that there is a marked difference between the two in that the expressions in *Heart of Darkness* are all 'abstract and extremely vague' and 'acquire evaluative connotations' (ibid). Stubbs' study is a good example of the different techniques available for text internal exploration, as well as for comparative analyses with reference to other corpora.

In terms of electronic explorations of literary texts, we can distinguish between two basic types of approaches; those that rely on intra-textual analysis and those that are based on comparisons of texts with reference to other collections of electronic texts:

- Intra-textual analysis is the manipulation of a text or text collections in a way that might reveal further information about the data, and assist in the interpretation process. This process is particularly useful when we consider longer texts and text collections. The type of manipulation we decide to carry out can be informed by existing interpretations, e.g. a concordance search of words that signal the theme of vagueness, which may have been previously identified, or it can be an exploration of the data that is not guided by previous readings, such as a frequency list of individual words and their collocates for example.

- Another approach is the comparison of individual lexical items and phrases in literary texts with those that occur in other, possibly non-literary, corpora with the aim of analysing deviations and their status as literary effects. This approach might include the analysis of collocations and semantic prosodies, for example. Reference corpora serve as a resource to establish language norms in this context. As such, they can be used as evidence to establish the meaning of individual words and phrases in general language use, which in turn can inform the analysis of such items in a literary text or corpus.

Both approaches can reveal useful information about the text, which might be used to complement other methods of analysis and challenge or support previous interpretations. The two approaches will be considered in more detail in the next sections.

Intra-textual analysis

One of the key differences between electronic text analysis and corpus linguistics, as highlighted in chapter one, is that a corpus tends to consist of more than one text and, because of its considerable size, it is often impossible to get to know all of its texts in the same way as you would be able to with a single novel for example. However, even when an individual text is sufficiently short to carry out some part of the analysis without computational help, the techniques covered in the previous two chapters can be useful tools in the context of analysing even a single text.

Apart from simple concordance and collocation analyses, the electronic analysis of literary texts may draw on any of the techniques introduced in the previous two chapters, including frequency lists of individual words and phrases, keyword analyses and calculations of type-token ratios.

Barnbrook (1996: 52), for example, shows how the frequency lists of *Frankenstein* can be analysed with a view to extracting all nouns that might refer to Frankenstein's creations, including for example *monster* and *creature*. A frequency wordlist can be easily scanned for such items and further concordance searches can be used to differentiate individual instances further according to their context of use.

A concordance search of a protagonist's name will provide an immediate 'picture' of the actions and feelings that occur in the textual vicinity of this character. The way in which a character is depicted in a story is often expressed in the verbs and adverbs that illustrate his or her actions and in the adjectives that are used to describe the person. A simple concordance search can often provide us with a general idea of how a character is presented in a story, or what recurrent actions or features are associated with a particular character.

The following selected lines have been extracted from Tolstoy's novel Anna Karenina.[1] Set in 1860s St Petersburgh society, Anna Karenina is the story of a passionate and impulsive woman driven ultimately to suicide by the impossible tension between her role as dutiful wife and mother, and her passion for Count Vronsky:

	Anna	
in love with older and married women.	**Anna**	did not resemble a fashionable lady
and attracted Kitty. Kitty felt that	**Anna**	was perfectly simple and was
she saw the charming figure and head of	**Anna**	in a black velvet gown. And he was
you always look the loveliest of all."	**Anna**	had the faculty of blushing. She
And to her surprise Dolly saw that	**Anna**	was blushing up to her ears, up to
in, asserting that her way was best, and	**Anna**	had become so heated that she blushed
dog when it has done wrong.	**Anna**	smiled- and her smile was
said Alexei Alexandrovich sternly.	**Anna**	smiled. She knew that he said this
he answered. "A most remarkable book."	**Anna**	smiled, as people smile at the
it." And, in spite of all her emotion,	**Anna**	smiled, as she caught the naive
said Alexei Alexandrovich sternly.	**Anna**	smiled. She knew that he said this
of a dark night. On seeing her husband,	**Anna**	raised her head and smiled, as
you said that!" said Dolly, laughing.	**Anna**	was hurt. "Oh no, oh no! I'm not
as he supposes." "Why can't they?"	**Anna**	said, restraining her tears, and
a baronetcy, and an estate, and	**Anna**	was feeling a desire to go with
were quite indifferent to her leaving.	**Anna**	was absorbed the whole morning in
her son, like her husband, aroused in	**Anna**	a feeling akin to disappointment.
him!" "No," Dolly was beginning, but	**Anna**	cut her short, kissing her hand on
he will marry Kitty." "Yes?" said	**Anna**	softly. "Come now, let us talk of

Anna's portrayal as a woman of passion and fleshly desires is emphasized by recurring descriptions of what she wears, as well as how she blushes and conveys her emotions. While further analyses of the personal pronoun *she* and of other forms of reference for her would have to be carried out to achieve a more comprehensive picture, the concordance lines above can be used to collect evidence for a possible portrait of Anna. We learn not only about her emotions, but also about her exterior: she is a simple woman who does not dress in a fashionable manner.

This type of analysis not only allows for an initial description of individual protagonists but also for comparisons between two characters or between the portrayal of gender groups for example. Kettemann (1995) demonstrates how to use this kind of research to highlight the different characterization of men and women in an early, emancipatory American short story. He runs concordances of the personal pronouns *she* and *he* and finds that at the beginning of the story *she* collocates mainly with housekeeping verbs, such as *cooking* and *baking* for example, while the verbs following *he* clearly denote a more varied class of lexical choice, making the male character appear more confident and in control. However, the roles of the characters change during the course of the story so that the concordance lines towards the end present a somewhat different picture. The verbs collocating with *she* at this later point in the narration have become more varied and convey the overall feeling of control, while those actions associated with *he* illustrate speechlessness and immobilization.

It should be noted, however, that this type of analysis can only be used to support very basic interpretations as it is not always apparent from the short span of a concordance line who is responsible for a particular judgement, whether it is the narrator or one of the other characters for example. A further investigation of the surrounding text can therefore be necessary, and the concordance tool can facilitate a direct display of the text that surrounds a particular concordance for this very purpose. It is also important to bear in mind that the concordance lines above have been selected to support a particular interpretation and that other concordance lines may give rise to different interpretations.

The distribution of individual lexical items can be represented visually in some software packages.[2] This allows the analyst to see at which point particular terms, such as names for example, or those items that relate to core themes in a literary text, are introduced, and whether they cluster at any point during the course of the text. This type of representation is maybe more appropriate to a single text rather than to a text collection, which contains a number of texts that are not arranged in any particular order.

Inter-textual analysis

The study of inter-textuality tends to refer to a level of textual reading that takes into account allusions to other texts known to the reader, for example religious or historical texts and which thus create a particular literary effect. Corpus linguistic techniques can be used to facilitate inter-textual analysis on a number of levels. One way, of course, is to run concordance searches of specific words and phrases from a literary text in the relevant texts and corpora that are alluded to, such as the electronic version of the bible in the case of some religious references. However, intertextuality comprises of the entire language experience of the reader and thus includes reference to the meaning and use of everyday vocabulary. Corpora can therefore also be used to analyse the meaning of individual words and phrases in a literary text with reference to everyday language use. This method might be particularly useful in the analysis of relatively short literary texts where, due to the limited number of instances of words and phrases in the actual text, a description of patterns in the text is not feasible.

A fruitful area of study in this context seems to be that of semantic prosody. As discussed in chapter four, the concept of 'semantic prosodies' describes the shading of individual words based on recurring patterns in large scale corpora and thus allows for an assessment of the connotations of individual items that is based on recurrent associations of such items in general language use. The shading of a lexical item can be determined by looking at its collocates. As outlined in chapter four Stubbs (1996: 174), for example, demonstrates with the use of corpus data that the lexical item *cause* regularly co-occurs with negative and unpleasant events. In the corpus he examines *accident*, *concern*, *damage*, *death* and *trouble* are the most common collocates of this verb. In the same way that it is difficult to determine semantic prosodies based solely on our intuition, it is also difficult for the writer or speaker to influence his or her choice of them. Thus Louw (1993: 157) argues that the study of semantic prosodies can be useful in uncovering 'the speaker's real attitude even where s/he is at pains to conceal it'. Examining the semantic prosody of the word 'utterly' in a Philip Larkin poem by examining its use in a corpus, Louw (1997) is able to illustrate the word's connotations of threat. This in turn contributes to the interpretation of the poem.

The use of corpus data to complement existing analytical frameworks and readings of literary texts in the ways outlined above highlights the potential of this approach. The next section will illustrate an example of how existing frameworks of speech and thought presentation in literary texts can be complemented by drawing on the analysis of semantic prosodies.

An example: semantic prosodies and point of view in fiction

In narrative fiction, the study of 'point of view' and the related aspect of speech and thought presentation have become a powerful means of establishing a systematic stylistic analysis of a text.

The way in which the characters' speech and thoughts are presented plays a major part in identifying the perspective from which a story is told, i.e. whether we are dealing with narrator or reflector mode. Simpson (1993: 21) thus argues that the stylistic analysis of speech and thought presentation, 'straddles the gap between spatio-temporal point of view and psychological point of view'.

The stylistic analysis of speech and thought presentation in narratives allows us to judge narratorial involvement in a story. The various grammatical structures which are used to present speech and thought can be arranged on a cline. Direct speech shows a high degree of character involvement while more indirect forms indicate an enhanced presence of the narrator who is 'telling' the reader what is happening. Leech and Short (1981) distinguish between five categories of speech and thought presentation, respectively, which are listed with examples on the cline below:

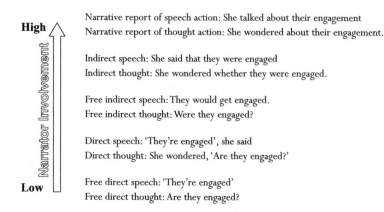

Narrative report of speech action: She talked about their engagement
Narrative report of thought action: She wondered about their engagement.

Indirect speech: She said that they were engaged
Indirect thought: She wondered whether they were engaged.

Free indirect speech: They would get engaged.
Free indirect thought: Were they engaged?

Direct speech: 'They're engaged', she said
Direct thought: She wondered, 'Are they engaged?'

Free direct speech: 'They're engaged'
Free direct thought: Are they engaged?

(based on Leech and Short 1981)

It becomes clear from the examples above that the omission of reporting clauses in the 'free' forms can make the assignment of narratorial perspective somewhat difficult. With thought presentation in particular, it is not always easy to distinguish between the 'reflector', i.e. the character whose thoughts are represented and comments from the narrator. The syntactic similarities of free indirect speech and free indirect thought add further to this complication, since we cannot always be sure who is speaking or indeed whether a character is speaking or thinking.

The grammatical structures which an author chooses to represent the speech and thoughts of characters in a piece of writing thus affect meaning and point of view. A further layer of meaning analysis can be achieved through the study of semantic prosodies. This will be illustrated with an extract from Virginia Woolf's *To the Lighthouse*, a text that is particularly interesting in terms of the linguistic representation of the characters' points of view and their attitudes towards one another.[3]

As a concept in stylistic analysis point of view embraces both the 'viewing position' in relation to a story, i.e. the perspective from which the narration originates, and the attitude of a character, or a focalizer, towards a particular aspect of the plot. A distinction is generally made between a first person and a third person narration, which we find in the extract at hand. A third person narration can be told either from the narrator's perspective or from the reflector's perspective, i.e. from an outside point of view or from the perspective of a character within the story. Within the two modes, narrator and reflector, Simpson (1993) distinguishes between three further types of point of view polarities, positive, negative and neutral, based on the types of modality that are used within the narration. In linguistics, modality refers to the way speakers express the possibility of or certainty in particular conditions. Propositions can be classified according to whether they express obligation, possibility, desire or belief, and these different classifications determine the 'shading' of a text. Positive shading is achieved through deontic or boulomaic modality, which denote the degree of obligation, commitment or desire in a proposition. This can be expressed through the use of modal auxiliaries, such as *will*, *must*, *can*, *should*, *may* or *would*, as in 'She must go', and modal adverbs, such as *possibly*, *probably* or *definitely*, *as in* 'She will definitely go'. Evaluative adjectives and adverbs, such as *beautiful* or *happy*, are further indications of positive modality shading. Negative shading is achieved by epistemic and perception modality, which convey the speaker's confidence in the truth of a proposition, as in the sentence 'I *think* she has left'. The last type of polarity, neutral modality shading, refers to a text in which modality is minimal and in which the narration is maybe at its most 'objective'.

Simpson considers the positive or negative shading that is conveyed by the different types of modality discussed above, in relation to the orientation towards the reader. The uncertainty that is transmitted through the use of epistemic modal adverbs such as 'possibly' or 'probably' for example 'render the events of the narrative less palpable' (Simpson 1993: 56).

However, rather than attaching 'shades' of modality intuitively to individual lexical items, the study of semantic prosodies allows for an empirical account of such shadings based on corpus evidence. As such, we could argue that 'uncertainty' is one aspect of the semantic prosody of epistemic modal verbs or adverbs. In a discussion of the word *just*, McCarthy (1998: 22) argues that the semantic prosody of the modal verbs that precede this item signals 'tentativeness/indirectness/face saving'. However, it is not only markers of modality that can be analysed in terms of their semantic prosody. The following analysis will focus on a range of lexical items to determine the effect of semantic prosodies on the narration.

Introduction to the text

Virginia Woolf's novel *To the Lighthouse* tells the story of the Ramsay family and their guests on an island in the Hebrides. The sentences discussed below are taken from an 'interaction' between Mrs Ramsay and her husband that takes place in one of the rooms in the holiday home. She is knitting a stocking while he is reading a book.[4] The narratorial style of *To the Lighthouse* is closely related to one of its main themes – that of vision and consciousness. One of the central questions put to the reader is: 'Out of that complex of retrospect and anticipation which is consciousness, what knowledge can emerge, what vision can be achieved [...] ?' (Daiches 1970: 93). A stylistic analysis of point of view in the extract below will contribute to our understanding of the 'vision' of a character with respect to both the situation and other characters.

Analysis

The extract begins in indirect thought mode, which takes the reader straight into Mrs Ramsay's thought process. Mrs Ramsay is the reflector; it is from her point of view that the story is told:

> What had happened she wondered, as she took up her knitting, since she had last seen him alone?

The presence of the narrator only becomes apparent in the reporting clause *she wondered*. The modality shading is negative, conveyed through the epistemic modal lexical verb *wondered*, which in turn mirrors the reflector's uncertainty. However, since the perception modality used in this sentence is part of the narrator's presence, a further indication is needed to assign uncertainty to the reflector's thoughts as such. This becomes possible through an analysis of the semantic prosody of the lexical item *happen*. Consider the concordance lines below, which represent a random sample of the word *happen* that occur in the *CANCODE* corpus:

not expecting an accident to	**happen**	as a matter of course but if
what sort of accident could	**happen**	then the slightly more likely one
so what's the worst that can	**happen**?	
ever known what was going to	**happen**	next she has to work it out as
something ridiculous would	**happen**.	
So what did you expect to	**happen**	when you complained?
never know what's going to	**happen**.	
much doubt anything's gonna	**happen**	to her.
It shouldn't	**happen**	again.
Saying please don't let that	**happen**.	
mean I witnessed an accident	**happen**	down the road car accident which
worry that the same might	**happen**	to the N H S we may not be able
didn't know what was gonna	**happen**	so em she had a better chance so
time you don't want it to	**happen**	anyway.
Knowing our luck it would	**happen**.	

We can see from these concordance lines that there are two main slants to the semantic prosody of this verb. The first one is that of uncertainty, which is conveyed mainly through the use of modality directly preceding *happen*. This sense of uncertainty is strongly related to people's negative expectations of past or future events (*the worst that can happen*, *worry that the same might happen*, *something ridiculous would happen*). The second aspect of the semantic prosody hence lies in the negative nature of concepts that habitually surround the word *happen*. Sinclair (1991: 112), in a discussion of the negative semantic prosody of *happen*, finds that the word *accident* is one of its main collocates. The negative shading, conveyed by the type of epistemic modality used by the narrator, is complemented by the uncertainty expressed through the character's thoughts, which can be seen as an indication of the blurring of narrator and character. The same prosody applies to the past tense form that is used in the extract from *To the Lighthouse* above:

the bang and gone to see what	**had happened**.	He was just coming
And she said something terrible	**had happened**	to her so I asked her what
because nobody could believe what	**had happened**.	Mm. Shock.
had happened something bad	**had happened**.	You know it was like
other horror stories about things that	**had happened**.	Cos I thought that it
basic problem could not be dealt with it	**had happened**.	Mm.
But I'd phone to check that nothing	**had happened**	in the day while they
not have been so good if bad things	**had happened**.	Yeah. We were
that that that nothing terrible	**had happened**	that my application was
And. You were late so what	**had happened**.	Oh yeah.

Again this concordance output shows the negative prosody that emerges from the language choices surrounding the grammatical structure *had happened*.

To illustrate the value of analysing semantic prosodies in this context, consider the next sentence, which occurs shortly after the one discussed above:

Her mind was still going up and down, up and down with poetry; he was still feeling very vigorous, very forthright, after reading about Steenie's funeral.

The cognitive action described in the first part of this sentence is likely to be the narrator's comment using Mrs Ramsay as the focalizer. The negativity and uncertainty in her mind and thus in the narratorital style continues, which can be illustrated via an analysis of the semantic prosody of the repeated prepositional cluster 'up and down'. There are, of course, several meanings of this phrase, most of which are related to physical movement and some of which are part of the phrase *to look someone up and down*. Where *up and down* refers to physical movement it tends to be positive in prosody, such as when it occurs as part of the phrase *to jump up and down*, referring here to children's activities. However, in those cases in which *up and down* refers to a person's state of mind, and sometimes in those where *up and down* refers metaphorically to movement, the prosody is one of uncertainty, often with an additional slant of negativity, as the small sample of concordance lines selected from the *CANCODE* corpus below illustrates:

running	**up and down**	the garden barking his head
me of the mad people that go	**up and down**.	
just be horrible like walking	**up and down**	in a ward when you're in pain
It seems to be it goes	**up and down**	and Mark gets it and doesn't
+they're both quite	**up and down**	and she's+
+stalking	**up and down**.	
Oh well it will go	**up and down**	yeah.
My employment is sort of	**up and down**	you know.

my stomach just kept going	**up and down**	didn't it bloating up and
She's	**up and down**	like a yo-yo.
So I suppose it went	**up and down**	a bit.
Oh yeah he goes	**up and down**	nobody's business.
moment cos he's so sort of	**up and down**	and not sure how he's gonna
And it's been up and down	**up and down**	sometimes it's got worse som
I've been	**up and down**	on it.

The phrase *up and down*, in emotional terms, is used to express an uncertain state of mind, often with a negative association. The 'prosodic clash' (Louw 1993) between the negative prosody of 'up and down' and the positive associations of the word 'poetry' may, on first reading, conceal the overall negative shading, which is yet another argument for the study of semantic prosodies as an integral part of a stylistic analysis. Looking at the concordance output of the word poetry in the CANCODE corpus we find that this concept often carries positive associations as illustrated in the selected lines below:

and wrote four prize winning volumes of er	**poetry**	er between the years nineteen
poetry I know Sarah yeah. The real	**poetry**.	Yeah. Come with me
some quality painting. Painting.	**Poetry**.	Yeah. Rambo.
Er she subsequently went on to write	**poetry**	and wrote four prize winning
brilliant. If you could put that in a line of	**poetry**	it'd be perfect wouldn't it?
process underlying. There is the	**poetry**	of the mind and that's logic as

There are also examples where the word poetry is used in connection with a negative evaluation, in particular when it is used in relation to a time period, country or writer.

The focalization changes after the first semicolon. We are here presented with the feelings and internal thought processes of Mr Ramsay. This change in focalization also marks a shift towards a more positive shading of the text. This is introduced by the verb *feeling*, which marks an internal emotional process: 'he was still *feeling* vigorous,…'. A further analysis of the semantic prosody of the lexical items that are used to describe Mr Ramsay's state of mind, *vigorous* and *forthright*, supports this hypothesis. Consider the following concordance lines taken from the BNC online service:[5]

A6C 487 Certainly my mother's successful campaign to have the nearby men's urinal closed was **vigorous** and rewarding.

ABF 788 It was a **vigorous** performance that went down well with a public that is feeling a mite embarrassed about not putting its money where America's mouth was once so loud.

BMN 2298 Corbett looked down at the fearful remains of a young man who, the last time they had met, had been a **vigorous** young soldier interested in clearing his own name.

C8A 227 **Vigorous** enjoyment

EA6 1032 from the late 1850s, however, a **vigorous** subculture, generating a series of revolutionary organizations, took root within Russia's privileged élite.

FU8 497 "I'm glad to meet you, Monsieur Devraux," cried Nathaniel Sherman, treating the Frenchman to warm, **vigorous** handshake.

HTM 504 I felt **vigorous**; my work fascinated me; I remained handsomely potent —;'; He smiled and shook his head at his own unspoken memories.

K9J 84 ';We set about a **vigorous** reconstruction programme supported by the ICI Group.

A corpus-based analysis of the word *vigorous* shows that, when it refers to humans, its prosody is almost consistently positive, as the examples above demonstrate. A similar pattern can be observed with the word *forthright*, as illustrated by the selected concordance lines below, also extracted via the BNC online service:

AD2 1073 A strong and **forthright** stand will continue to be taken in accordance with Christian principles on the great moral issues of our day.

BNS 933 A woman of such **forthright** views as yourself would, I feel, lend considerable weight to this project.

CBG 9269 While Graeme is certainly a very opinionated and **forthright** personality, he seemed more aloof from the players to me.

CCC 1853 The electrical power workers, however, did not respond in the **forthright** way they had done in the general strike of May 1974.

CD2 2531 George, the second son, more **forthright** and readily spoken, was put to selling insurances with an acquaintance of Lessing's.

CH8 1959 Why should he —; he has his own career, his own life and he's pretty **forthright** on many things —; and a very good thing, too.

EVH 1457 He gave confidence by being **forthright**.

F9W 686 We often say more than we need, perhaps to mark a sense of occasion, or respect; and we often say less than we need, perhaps to be rude, or blunt, or **forthright**.

FPK 897 Luther knew that he might search long and hard, from one end of the earth to the other, but he would never find such an incredibly **forthright** and loyal employee.

G2E 2808 Now that the Sun is passing through your own birth sign, you are certain to be at your most **forthright**, purposeful and ready to go into battle at the slightest provocation.

GUF 1830 He was a **forthright** man who made enemies, but was loved and respected by his friends.

KAE 78 Nevertheless, she is delightfully **forthright**, alert and amusing.

Although the semantic prosody of *forthright*, when it refers to humans, is maybe less positive than that of *vigorous* and often associated with bluntness and direct-ness, it nevertheless clearly denotes confidence and certainty about one's own views and opinions. It is hence often used to describe people in political contexts, with a majority of these being male. The semantic prosodies of *forthright* and *vigorous* stand thus not only in sharp contrast to the description used for Mrs Ramsay's frame of mind, *up and down*, but also introduce a shift in the point of view that is being described. Both *vigorous* and *forthright* are highly evaluative, thus denoting positive shading according to Simpson's (1993) model.

What is striking in the analysis above is the shifting of modes; between direct and indirect, between the reflector's thoughts and the narrator's comments and between speech and thought. The blurring of speech and thought brings out one of the main themes in the novel: the discrepancy between 'conception and articula-tion' (Davies 1989: 18).

Concluding remarks

The analysis of semantic prosodies in the extract from *To the Lighthouse* brings out the differences in the 'shading' of the text, which tends towards uncertainty and negativity in the depiction of Mrs Ramsay's character and towards strength and certainty in the case of Mr Ramsay. This, in turn, underlines the analysis of point of view in the novel. Further subdivisions to Simpson's (1993) model could thus be suggested which depend on the 'shading' of the text achieved through the semantic prosodies of individual lexical items.

The analysis above is meant to be illustrative rather than comprehensive and has thus focused on a limited sample of two sentences. However, the annotation of lit-erary corpora makes it possible to study analytical categories, such as speech and thought presentations, in a systematic way. The next section deals with the kind of annotation that is required for such an analysis.

Annotating literary corpora for stylistic research

One of the advantages of drawing on methodologies from the area of electronic text analysis as an approach to literary texts is that particular textual features can be made more visible through systematic annotation. Annotation and mark-up processes discussed in chapter two, can range from unanalysed elements, such as the mark-up of different speakers in a drama for example, to more complex anno-tations of particular analytical categories, such as different types of speech and thought presentation. The former can be done automatically with specially designed software programmes (see van-Oskam and Zundert 2004) or manually. Standard automatic annotation of linguistic elements, such as parts of speech for example, are of course also possible with literary corpora, and can facilitate the identification of particular grammatical categories.

The annotation of analytical categories in literary texts tends to be carried out manually as they require a complex process of identification by a trained researcher. There is currently no software program that could automatically annotate different types of speech and thought presentation in literary texts. In a recent book on corpus stylistics, Semino and Short (2004) illustrate an annotation scheme for a revised version of the speech and thought presentation framework developed by Leech and Short (1981). The authors construct a corpus of narrative texts consisting of prose fiction, newspaper news reports and (auto)biography, which allows them to carry out comparisons between the different patterns of speech and thought presentation found in the respective genres. Although the corpus for this project is relatively small, with just under 260,000 words, the careful annotation of speech and thought presentation make this an invaluable resource, since it produces quantifiable evidence of different narrator styles, and is thus unique for testing hypotheses in this area.

The annotated corpus developed for this project can be used for both quantitative and qualitative comparisons. The quantitative analysis, for example, includes comparisons of overall numbers of occurrences of the different categories of speech and thought presentation in the different genres and sub-genres, and mean word-length of individual speech and thought categories in the corpus. The authors are able to demonstrate significant differences between categories by drawing on log-likelihood statistics (see chapter three). The systematic analysis of the different categories also allows the extraction of speech and thought reporting verbs and for a comparison between such verbs in different genres.

As outlined in chapter two, any type of manual annotation that relies on processes of initial interpretation of the text is by definition subjective, at least to a degree. In order to ensure that the annotation is sufficiently stable and consistent with a particular theoretical framework, it can be useful to carry out an inter-rater reliability test, whereby two or more researchers annotate the same data independently with the aim of assessing the level of consistency in the emerging annotation. This process can also be valuable as the basis for a refinement of analytical categories.

Summary

This chapter has provided a brief and introductory overview of the different types of explorations that become possible through the electronic analysis of literary texts. These have included discussions of individual texts, as well as analyses of individual items in reference corpora. The use of corpus linguistic techniques in this area is still relatively new and more research is needed to assess the full potential of this approach.

However, the different types of analysis introduced in this chapter have illustrated a way of gathering evidence that is needed to test particular hypotheses in relation to literary texts. In addition, it has been demonstrated how corpus linguistic analyses of semantic prosodies might be used as part of a wider analysis of point of view in a text, and how this type of exploration contributes to our understanding of the way in which the meaning of individual lexical items contributes to the textual orientation towards the reader.

Activities

1. When literary texts are put into electronic format they can be subjected to electronic text analysis. In this chapter we have seen how character description and the study of point of view in literary texts can be complemented by electronic text analysis. Can you think of any other areas in the study of literature which would benefit from an intra-textual corpus-based approach and why?

2. The study of semantic prosodies has been used to analyse irony in texts. Irony is here seen in terms of a clash between an expected semantic profile of a lexical item and its semantic prosody in a particular instance of usage. We would expect for example that the word 'fine' has positive attributes in use. Louw (1993) shows that this is generally the case unless it precedes words which describe family members or friends, such as 'He is a *fine* friend', in which case it tends to express irony. A concordance search of the word 'fine' in a general corpus of English will uncover this pattern. Can you find an example of irony in a text which works on a clash of semantic prosodies?

3. Miall (1996), drawing on Van Peer (1989), points out that 'the frequencies of words, collocations, or particular stylistic features, tell us rather little about the literary qualities of a text, since these aspects of a text find their meaning only within the larger and constantly shifting context constituted by the reading process. Text as object (a pattern of words) is a quite different entity from text as communication (a reader's interaction with a text)'. Discuss the role of 'reader response' in relation to electronic text analysis.

Further reading

A discussion of corpus approaches to literary texts can be found in Stubbs (2005), Kettemann (1995) and Semino and Short (2004). The notion of *semantic prosody* is discussed in Sinclair (2004a: chapter 2) and Stubbs (1996), and its application to literary texts has been developed by Louw (1993). For a critique of the use of computational methods in literary studies see Miall (1995) and Van Peer (1989).

The role of point of view in literary texts has been discussed extensively in the literature on stylistics (see for example Rimmon-Kenan 1983). Genette (1980) provides an influential framework to analyse narrative discourse. Simpson (1993) presents the notion of point of view in an accessible framework and also introduces the different aspects of modality shading in texts. The related concept of speech and thought presentation is developed in Leech and Short (1981) and Short (1996).

Notes

1. The concordance search was generated via the interactive website of the Oxford Text Archive at <http://ota.ox.ac.uk/>.
2. *Wordsmith Tools* for example can generate this type of representation.
3. Part of this analysis is based on Adolphs and Carter (2002).
4. Woolf (1964 [1927]), *To the Lighthouse*, p. 140.
5. See <http://sara.natcorp.ox.ac.uk/lookup.html>.

6 Electronic text analysis, language and ideology

Introduction

Since language is the key vehicle for the expression of ideology, the analysis of corpus data lends itself to this area of research. This chapter explores in more detail how the electronic analysis of texts can aid the study of ideology. In the previous chapter we have seen how the study of point of view in narrative fiction may be complemented with an investigation of semantic prosodies of individual lexical items and phrases. The same technique has been used to analyse the manifestation of ideology in everyday spoken and written discourse and particular reference will be made to the concept of semantic prosody during this chapter. It has a particular place in the study of ideology, as it facilitates the description of individual words and phrases in terms of their positive or negative shading.

Language, ideology and corpora

The term ideology has been used to refer both to dogmatic positions especially in the context of political agendas, and to sets of individual and collective beliefs (see de Beaugrande 1999, Wodak 1996). The study of ideology within the areas of critical linguistics (Fowler *et al.* 1979) and critical discourse analysis (Fairclough 1989, 1992) focuses on uncovering unequal relations of power through the close analysis of language used to represent certain aspects of society.

It can often be difficult to uncover ideology in texts purely on the basis of intuition, and different people may 'read' and interpret the same text in a different manner. Critical discourse analysts draw on a number of linguistic frameworks, including those that have been developed in the area of pragmatics, narratology and systemic functional linguistics (see Halliday 1985) to counteract inequality and dominance expressed through language by making the linguistic traces that support these processes more explicit. Ideology is here used in a negative sense, relating to the goal of enforcing unequal power relationships, and pertaining mainly to those types of discourses that pursue this goal. However, there are certain problems associated with linking ideology to particular types of discourse only. De Beaugrande (1999) argues that the selection of the types of texts that reproduce a certain ideology requires a conceptualization of that ideology that is not based on textual analysis, and thus may, in itself, involve subjective judgement of some kind. A more neutral interpretation of the term ideology as a set of beliefs allows for a more inclusive study of different types of discourses, and gets around the problem of subjective choice of texts to some extent. It also allows us to take a broader view of ideology, which may include the study of domination and unequal power relationships, but also a more general representation of counter-ideologies, that may become apparent through the study of corpus data (ibid).

The electronic analysis of texts and text collections provides an approach to this area which is well placed to complement more traditional frameworks used in critical discourse analysis, as well as to be used in its own right. Working with large amounts of texts has the advantage of providing a substantial amount of evidence that can be used to support interpretations of language use. This makes the analysis less subjective, and allows for discussions of different types of ideologies as they emerge from the data. Finally, there is a practical benefit to the use of electronic text analysis and the use of corpus analytical techniques in this context. The study of frequency lists, concordance outputs and keywords makes it possible to compare large text collections in a relatively short amount of time.

Since the study of ideology with the use of large scale corpus data is still very much in the early stages, there is a real need for a better understanding of the processes that make us choose particular words or phrases for our analysis, how we assign semantic prosodies and interpret concordance outputs in this context, and how the analysis of corpus data may interface with more traditional approaches to critical discourse analysis. At the same time, we need to acknowledge the effect of using de-contextualized data in this area of study. Analysing individual concordance lines without reference to the text from which they originate, or indeed, the particular passage of text that surrounds them, may affect our analysis in a way that makes it difficult to make statements about traces of ideology in a language.

In the meantime, there is a growing body of research that illustrates the usefulness of the type of evidence we are able to collect through electronic text analysis in the study of ideology. The analysis of semantic prosody has been a particular focus in this context and the remainder of this chapter will explore this particular area of research in more depth.

Electronic texts for the study of ideology

Before we move on to a more detailed exploration of semantic prosodies and ideology, we will briefly consider the issue of research design in this context. When it comes to the study of ideology, the choice of texts is probably the most important factor in the research design process. After all, the main aim is to uncover the stance taken by an individual or a group of individuals towards other members or issues in a society.

Cook (2004) shows how we can identify and describe traces of ideology in language with reference to the on-going debate of genetically modified food. In his book on *Genetically Modified Language*, he makes a useful distinction between 'the speakers', 'the spoken about' and 'the spoken to'. The three elements of what Cook calls the 'triangle of communication' are necessarily interdependent in that the topic, or 'the spoken about' is linked to the speakers and the prospective audience, or the 'spoken to'. Depending on which particular angle of ideology is being studied, this three-partite division can be used as a framework for corpus design.

If you are interested in the ideology conveyed by a particular speaker or author, you would collect a corpus that includes samples of the discourse of that particular person. Flowerdew (1997), for example, studies the speeches of Chris Patten, who was the last British governor of Hong Kong. Flowerdew explores the lexical environment of words related to Patten's political agenda, such as *economy* for example, and analyses the semantic prosody that emerges through collocational patterns. The widespread use of the internet today means that a vast amount of political discourse is now freely available to download, including party manifestos, speeches and pamphlets. These can be turned into corpora and explored electronically in order to uncover particular ideologies (see, for example, Fairclough's (2000) analysis of the British Prime Minister Tony Blair's speeches).

Traces of ideology in the language of individual speakers can also be studied with reference to large-scale corpora of general English. Cook (2004), for example, studies a speech given by Tony Blair on GM food in 2002. In his speech, Blair uses the phrase 'overrun by protestors and pressure groups', which prompts Cook to analyse the phrase 'overrun by' in the *COBUILD* corpus. The concordance output for 'overrun by' shows that this phrase commonly co-occurs with words that have a negative semantic prosody, such as *fire* and *mourners*, or that are used to refer to potential enemies of Britain, such as *Iraqi troops* for example. Cook (2004: 16) concludes that Tony Blair's use of the phrase 'overrun by' in conjunction with *protestors* and *pressure groups* shows that he assigns the same negative quality to them.

It is, of course, also possible to analyse the language of a group of speakers. For example, if you are interested in contrasting the ideology surrounding the term 'immigration' in tabloid versus broadsheet newspaper articles, you would collect a corpus that includes samples of these general 'speaker' divisions and articles on the topic of immigration.

In order to explore the 'spoken about', it can be useful to refer to a large-scale reference corpus, such as the *BNC* for example. This will allow you to study how particular terms are used in general English. We will see in more detail in the sample analysis carried out below what such a study might look like.

If your point of departure is the 'spoken to' element, you might want to assemble a corpus of texts that you know are written explicitly for a particular audience (such as academic journals for example). We would expect to find differences in the representation of particular issues, depending on whether the discourse has been written for a specialist audience or a non-specialist audience. This might be reflected in differences in the language used in academic journals versus that used in popular journalism for example.

The study of ideology with the use of corpora requires a very detailed rationale for the chosen texts, as their origin is likely to influence the outcome of the analysis to a considerable degree. Furthermore, it is important to analyse deviations of patterns in some detail, as these may represent important nuances of a particular ideology. And finally, it is important to include some reference to the period during which the particular texts originated, as ideology can change over time.

Key words, grammatical structures and ideology

We have seen in chapter three how keywords can be derived statistically from a corpus. In this calculation, individual items or phrases in a text or a corpus are compared with the relative frequency of the same items in a much larger, reference corpus. Here, keywords are those words that occur with a significantly higher or significantly lower frequency in the particular corpus. However, the term 'key word' is often used in a different sense in studies of ideology in corpora. Here the term refers to lexical items or phrases that are closely related to the representation of ideology. As such, they are often identified intuitively as prime candidates that may facilitate the process of uncovering a certain type of ideology in language. De Beaugrande (1999), for example, studies concordance data of the term *liberal* and its derivatives in the *Bank of English*™ and in the Corpus of South African English. He identifies *liberal* as a key term in post-modern society, and the corpus resources he has chosen allow him to analyse the use of this term in British, American and South African English. Teubert (2000) draws on a similar technique for identifying keywords that are related to the language of Euroscepticism in Britain. He studies words such as *federal*, *corruption* and *independence* in a corpus of texts that express a negative attitude towards the European Union.

A possible criticism of the approach that identifies particular words intuitively for investigation is that this is inevitably done at the expense of other words in the respective texts or corpora, and we cannot be sure whether the study of other lexical items would support or contradict our analysis. It is important, therefore, not to jump to conclusions about a particular ideology of a speaker or set of speakers, based on the analysis of a limited set of intuitively selected lexical items. There are, of course, other ways of identifying particular lexical items that are not immediately prone to the same criticism. These include the statistical derivation of keywords discussed in chapter three, and the analysis of lexical items based on raw frequency lists. However, these procedures may not produce the same words that would be identified intuitively to have a particular significance in terms of their association with a particular ideology. A combined approach that considers statistically derived keywords, as well as other items selected because of their analytical relevance, and that discusses emerging results with due caution in relation to the respective limitations, can therefore be appropriate.

The following section will illustrate a detailed corpus analysis of some forms of the lemma GENE and the particular ideologies behind their use and understanding in the public domain.[1]

A sample analysis

Introduction

As outlined in the introduction to this chapter, the term 'ideology' can refer to different concepts, ranging from a particular political stance to a set of beliefs held by an individual or group of people. For the purpose of this sample analysis, the latter meaning is being used in that ideology here is understood as a relatively neutral term that relates to beliefs and attitudes. In this case, we are concerned with attitudes and beliefs as they emerge from general English in use on the particular issue of 'genetics'. While research into the public understanding of genetics has greatly expanded in recent years, there has been relatively little effort in linking corpus evidence to this area of investigation. The advantage of using this technique in such contexts lies in the unmediated nature of corpus data, which allows the analyst to tap into the way which certain words are used in real-life contexts.

The meaning of genetics: background

Despite the interest in genetics in many different fields now, a precise analysis of how people conceptualize the term *genes* and other related words has yet to take place. Gene talk is a fitting topic of analysis because it pervades our culture at present. Between 1953 and 2002 there have been tremendous changes in genetic science. Breakthroughs would include deciphering, in the 1950s and 1960s, what Watson and Crick called the human genetic 'code' (quoted in Nelkin 2001: 557) to cloning Dolly the sheep in 1997 or reporting the results of the Human Genome Project in 2000 and 2001 (Nerlich *et al.* 2002). However, despite these breakthroughs, our relation to biotechnology seems ambivalent, and we would expect our language to reflect this.

Previous research in this area has highlighted that public attitudes towards biotechnology, especially in Europe, are mostly negative (Marris *et al.* 2001). Additionally, advances in biotechnology frequently receive sceptical treatment in the media (Bauer and Gaskell 2002). We would therefore expect to find a negative semantic prosody of the lemma GENE in general corpora of English, which provide evidence for public attitudes. In essence, there is no better laboratory for studying people's understanding of genetic science than looking directly at the relevant words themselves, as they are used by members of the public.

Description of corpus data

Since the aim of this analysis is to develop an understanding of the set of beliefs associated with the notion of genetics, as displayed by the general public, it is important to draw on a range of text resources. The analysis of the word *gene* and its various derivations is based on a number of different corpora. These include two large-scale general corpora, the *British National Corpus* and the *Bank of English*™, as well as the *CANCODE* corpus, which offers a suitable resource for analysing spoken English in a range of different contexts.[2] While the large scale general corpora can provide overall frequency patterns of the different forms of the lemma GENE, and allow for an analysis of common collocates, it is the spoken data that is maybe most suitable in an analysis of public understanding of this term. This is because the spoken corpus consists of everyday, un-scripted conversations between a wide range of people, while the written corpora used here include material from different, and sometimes specialist, sources. As such, they do not necessarily reflect the beliefs and attitudes of the general public, but since they have been compiled with the general public as an audience, we can assume that they at least inform those attitudes to a certain extent.

The larger written corpora thus allow us to carry out more data intensive types of analysis, such as frequency counts and collocation analysis, while the spoken corpus acts as a resource for a more in-depth, qualitative analysis of how this particular term is used in everyday discourse.

The *CANCODE* corpus has been organized according to five context types, which represent a cline of formality and which thus enable an analysis of ideologies according to different discourse contexts. The framework of categorization is based on the relationship that holds between the speakers in the dyadic (two-way) and multi-party conversations in the corpus. These types of relationships fall into five broad categories, which were identified at the outset of compiling the corpus and subsequently refined: *intimate, socio-cultural, professional, transactional* and *pedagogic*. These categories were found to be largely exclusive whilst, at the same time, being comprehensive. In the *intimate* category the distance between the speakers is at a minimum, such as is the case in interactions between partners or family members. The *socio-cultural* category implies the voluntary interaction between speakers that seek each other's company for the sake of the interaction itself. The relationship between the speakers is usually marked by friendship and is thus not as close as that between speakers in the *intimate* category. Typical venues for this type of interaction are social gatherings, birthday parties, sports clubs and voluntary group meetings. The *professional* category refers to the relationship that holds between people who are interacting as part of their regular daily work. This category only applies to interactions where all speakers are part of the *professional* context. The *transactional* category embraces interactions in which the speakers do not previously know one another. The purpose behind transactional conversations is usually related to a particular need on the part of the hearer or the speaker. As such, the conversations aim to satisfy a particular transactional goal, such as buying and selling for example. The *pedagogic* category was set up to include any conversation in which the relationship between the speakers was defined by the pedagogic context. A range of tutorials, seminars and lectures were included.[3]

Data analysis

In order to uncover common public understanding of the variants of the lemma GENE, the following study includes three different types of analysis. First of all the different parts of this lemma are identified through a frequency count in one of the large written corpora. The distribution of the variants of the lemma in the different contextual categories of the spoken corpus are then considered. Finally, we consider an example of an extended stretch of discourse, where the participants are talking about the issue of genetics.

Frequencies

The different variants of the lemma GENE were identified in the *British National Corpus* (BNC World) and yielded the following frequencies: *gene* (2237 instances), *genes* (2069 instances), *genetic* (1823 instances), *genetically* (335 instances) and *genetics* (302 instances). The nouns *gene* and *genes* are clearly the most frequent representations of this lemma. They are closely followed by the adjective *genetic*. The frequency drops sharply when we consider the adverb *genetically*. The noun *genetics* has the lowest frequency. We will return to a discussion of these frequency counts at a later stage in the analysis, when we have established the overall meaning that is attached to the different variants of this lemma based on a concordance analysis.

While the *British National Corpus* offers a general picture of frequencies, we can turn to the *CANCODE* corpus to analyse frequencies according to different conversational contexts (see table 6.1).

These frequency results are interesting, as they give us an indication of the types of situations in which people discuss *genetics*. While we would expect these figures to be high in the pedagogic category, taking into account that a number of recorded interactions were medical and biology lectures and seminars, it is interesting to note that the area of genetics is also being discussed in interactions between close

Table 6.1 Frequencies of the lemma GENE in the CANCODE corpus according to speaker relationship category.

	Intimate	Socio-cultural	Professional	Transactional	Pedagogic
Gene	4	1		1	16
Genes	13	1			35
Genetic	6	5		2	44
Genetically	3				1
Genetics	2				3

friends and partners. It is exactly this type of social sphere, where unmediated, recorded conversations occur, which can offer us insights into public attitudes to genetics and we will return to this aspect below.[4]

Concordance data

If we consider the concordance lines taken from the intimate and the pedagogic category, it becomes clear that the term is used in different ways in the two categories:

Intimate:

It could be a	**genetic**	mutation.
same way that red hair was	**genetic**	programming which has skipped
But a	**genetic**	experiment cloning a naturally
mouse is vile and a foul	**genetic**	experiment.
just saying that it could be	**genetic**	programming.
Well they come out the same	**genetic**	they come out the same

Pedagogic:

you and I carry D N A as our	**genetic**	material and it's double-stranded
Three K Bs of	**genetic**	material.
the way viruses carry their	**genetic**	material.
If we get a change in	**genetic**	pool this can lead to a failure
Viruses consist of some	**genetic**	material whether it be R N A or
abnormalities or changes in	**genetic**	pool.

In the intimate category the adjective *genetic* pre-modifies the nouns *mutation*, *programming* and *experiment* and there is some evidence of a negative prosody in this sample (e.g. 'vile and foul genetic experiment'). The examples taken from the pedagogic category collocate with *material* and *pool*, and although they display a semantic preference agents and processes that can cause disease (e.g. *viruses, abnormalities* and *failure*), there seems to be no direct evaluation attached to them. It should be noted that we are dealing with a very limited data set here, which does not allow us to make any generalizations about the use of this lemma.

If we broaden our analysis to include concordance data from the *British National Corpus* and the *Bank of English*™, we find further evidence for the different types of interpretations made above. Here our analysis starts with the two most frequent items, the nouns *gene* and *genes*. Both often occur as first names and modifiers in complex noun phrases or as part of compound nouns (e.g. gene pool, gene therapy, gene activity, snail genes, gene code, etc.). In this form they tend to be used as extended metaphors. The contexts in which they are found are almost always scientific, which is mirrored by the semantic preference of biomedical vocabulary, as shown in the following selected examples taken from the Collins Wordbanks *Online* English corpus:

preserve Amazonia as a source of drugs or as a **gene** bank. What for? Its real importance is as a
government has approved the first therapeutic **gene** transfer treatment of humans. Scientists in
esearchers from Maryland and Tokyo took this **gene** hbx, from out of the rest of the virus and
It may be that other mutations of the same **gene** cause other forms of anti-social behaviour,"
Better start looking around for a **gene** pool. [p] By 10pm I was getting hungry enough
found that very simple computer models of **gene** networks displayed astonishingly efficient to
reproduce. Far more common are recessive- **gene** diseases, some of which I've listed in Table 2.
and I are long gone from it. [p] Wertheimer: **Gene** therapy experiments begin on humans today with
standing debate that delayed the application of **gene**- splicing technology in growing food. Peter

A similar pattern can be found when we consider the following concordance lines selected data from the *British National Corpus*:

A3Y 152 because they had inherited a faulty kinase **gene**.
AKF 26 what was good for a **gene** might not be good for an individual.
ANX 1493 How important are these **gene** transfer processes in the natural
ARR 1089 It may be that a **gene's** effects, as a matter of fact, turn out to be
ASL 21 Is there a **gene** for each nerve cell?
ASL 1102 If the **gene** is isolated then it can be cloned –; that is,
C9V 688 one wrong base pair in the DNA of the **gene** coding for a particular enzyme means that
CRM 21 sequences reveals that the single GGF **gene** encodes multiple Schwann cell mitogens

Collocation and semantic prosody

The same tendency of usage within scientific contexts emerges from an analysis of the 10 most significant lexical collocates of the different variants of the lemma derived from the Collins Wordbanks *Online* English corpus (see table 6.2).[5]

The collocates in table 6.2 give a good indication as to the different contexts of use, and at the same time illustrate a tendency towards a negative semantic prosody, realized in collocates such as *cancer* and *disease*. It should also be noted that one of the collocates of the word *genes* in the table above is the lexical item *cause*, which, as illustrated in chapter four, has a strongly negative semantic prosody, hinting at the pervasive popular belief that genes 'cause' disease or behaviour, commonly referred to as genetic determinism.

Table 6.2 Ten most significant lexical collocates of the lemma GENE in the Collins WordbanksOnline English corpus.

Collocates	Gene	Genes	Genetic	Genetically	Genetics
1	hackman	human	engineering	engineered	biology
2	therapy	other	material	modified	research
3	kelly	cells	defects	programmed	human
4	responsible	cell	research	been	biochemistry
5	sarazen	specific	disease	have	molecular
6	gene	disease	make	determined	behaviour
7	cancer	language	DNA	food	cancer
8	scientists	cause	factors	different	role
9	disease	inherit	environmental	foods	microbiology
10	called	inserted	differences	cells	genetics

A closer look at the concordance output in the Cobuild sampler reveals the general trend towards this prosody. It is interesting to note, however, that this trend is much more prominent with the lexical items *genetic* and *genetically* compared to *gene, genes* and *genetics*, which display a more neutral, scientific semantic prosody. The concordance lines below, which are taken from the BNC, illustrate this:

AE7 155 This could be caused either by a **genetic** change which altered the relevant attaching

B77 252 it backs increased monitoring of **genetic** damage in groups of humans, such as workers

C8B 614 of sufferers have some sort of **genetic** susceptibility to it, and three times as many

C94 1068 against the theory of the **genetic** susceptibility to certain diseases of different

EV6 1524 to monitor for **genetic** contamination (16).

FL6 199 know it's also a **genetic** pre-disposition to anorexia nervosa, in other

FT3 1269 In a detailed study of the **genetic** deletions found in colorectal cancer one of the

HH3 8342 Even a **genetic** predisposition to psychosis usually has to be

J18 1418 and lead to the problem of **genetic** erosion of the crop, and are also difficult to

AAP 45 scrutiny is the part dealing with **genetically** modified organisms (GMOs) Genetic

AAX 280 swallowed tomato seeds (of a **genetically** engineered wrinkle-free tomato) the

ABK 88 ancestors thought, that blacks are **genetically** inferior in the traits that count for

AHG 686 degenerate sub-species, **genetically** afflicted by feeble-mindedness, insanity,

B77 754 disease, transmitted between **genetically** susceptible people and occurring in

BMG 1559 a cat with a limp body that **genetically** lacks the usual defensive reactions of

BNA 892 people born under your sign are **genetically** hopeless at the job?

BPA 2739 A **genetically** constructed freak joining humanity to...

CGC 2077 An Arsenal player could be the **genetically** engineered bastard son of a dangerous

CMA into hostility when phrases like '; **genetically** programmed'; are used instead.

GUG 3865 was the virus priming itself **genetically**, like a tiny bacteriological time-bomb,

HXT 569 Britain are at risk of producing a **genetically** "diseased" baby.

When we consider the selected concordance lines, we see that the clash between the natural and the artificial here could not be clearer, the 'natural', in this case, referring to something that is not controlled, manipulated, modified, altered, programmed or engineered by human beings. All deviation from what is 'natural' strikes us as dangerous and something to be avoided. Nobody might have any concern for a bridge that was 'mechanically engineered' because of what we take the nature of engineering to be. However, when engineering meets biology, then concerns spring up because a tomato that is 'genetically engineered' is perhaps something to reconsider before dinner. The semantic prosody, therefore, reflects a limit of acceptability: we accept the fact that cars are engineered, but we have a harder time accepting the fact that tomatoes, too, can also be engineered.

If we consider the nouns *gene*, *genes* and *genetics* on the other hand, the concordance output shows that they are used more frequently in scientific contexts and with a more neutral prosody overall. This is illustrated in the concordance output of the word *gene* taken from the *BNC*.

ARR 1562 The important thing is that a	**gene**	for a stage in pathway 1 will flourish in the
ASL 21 Is there a	**gene**	for each nerve cell?
B71 1556 level of the neurone or of the	**gene**.	
B75 559 the expression of the myc	**gene**	–; and Croce and his collaborators reported
CNA 595 The penetrance of the dominant	**gene**	in adults was estimated at 0.26 hence the risk
CRM 5875 homologue (P) of the mouse p	**gene**,	and appears to encode an integral membrane
CRM 8618 Third, this	**gene**	encodes a putative protein-tyrosine kinase
EE8 329 sickle cell trait where the abnormal	**gene**	is inherited from one parent only had sickle
FTB 599 A candidate	**gene**	that could be regulated by N-Oct 3 is the
FTE 850 to H1, transcription of the H1t	**gene**,	like the H1, is not S-phase-dependent.
HU3 227 and mutation of the p53	**gene**	is now well described in large bowel cancer.
HWT 1097 mutations within the APC	**gene**	causing variations from a total absence of

Overall, we can conclude then that the semantic prosody is closely related to the grammatical role of the particular lexical item of this lemma. The adjective *genetic* and the adverb *genetically* give rise to a range of processes that reinforce the negative semantic prosody, such as *genetic modification* or *genetically engineered*. We could therefore argue that while there is a neutral, scientific voice to the discourse related to genetics in certain contexts, there are, at the same time, negative prosodies which are particularly prominent in the use of the lexical items *genetic* and *genetically*. The overall frequency analysis of the different variants of this lemma shows that the nouns *gene* and *genes* occur with a higher frequency than the other variants of this lemma. Following such an analysis it might be helpful to relate the usage of these items to the texts from which they are drawn. When we consider the scientific contexts in which the nouns occur in our analysis, we may well find that they are derived from a particular part of the overall corpus that consists of discourse relating to a scientific domain.

Extending the analysis to the level of discourse

At this stage, it might be useful to take a closer look at the extended discourse context in which the individual items occur. The extract from the *CANCODE* corpus below shows a young couple who are discussing one of the aspects in the debate surrounding *genetics*:

> <S01> I mean what he said was Yes I could agree with it. I'm not into altering natures like watching animals being
> <S02> Like genetically altered. Yeah.
> <S01> Yeah tha= That I don't go with. If you get bad ones then+
> <S02> Yeah.
> <S01> +you're meant to have bad ones+
> <S02> Mm.
> <S01> +in life. That's what makes life life isn't it? I mean it is sad when it's children but it is a It's been like this forever. And you start altering that then that that is not on to me. But yet I don't want to be told+
> <S02> Yeah.
> <S01> +over And about the crops and things. And he said And he said about you know "Buy them in the shops these. Always look for organically grown as well." And I said to your dad "Everybody should be". And I said "Oh yeah. People with not much money are certainly gonna go and+
> <S02> Yeah.
> <S01> +look for organically grown stuff." "It only costs a few pence more." I thought "And the rest". You know stuff is so dear.
> <S02> Yeah.

Here we see a representation of a negative attitude towards the process of *genetic altering* in a stretch of ongoing discourse that is conveyed in a series of statements of opinion (e.g. 'I'm not into altering natures', 'That I don't go with'). This type of discourse level analysis is thus helpful when it comes to contextualizing the use of a particular variant. However, further analyses of a wider range of discourse contexts would be necessary if we wanted to make any statements about emerging patterns of use at discourse level. The importance of going beyond the analysis of frequencies and concordance data will be discussed in more detail in the next section.

Dealing with exception

While corpus analysis is concerned with patterns rather than with isolated instances, it is important to deal with the exceptions to certain patterns in some detail. This is because they often give rise to additional meanings that may be related to a particular context of use for example. In the following instances, taken from all three corpora discussed above, the semantic prosody appears to be distinctly positive:

- genetic endowment
- genetic richness
- genetic diversity
- genetically pure
- genetically purer
- genetically superior
- gene therapy
- genes might have been nature's gift
- desirable genes.

There are at least two explanations for why a deviation from the pattern of either negative or neutral semantic prosody established above might occur. One is related to the discourse context, i.e. if we consider a corpus of the discourse produced by speakers who are in favour of genetic engineering, then we are likely to find a change in the semantic prosody of this term. Since the corpora discussed as part of this analysis are all designed to capture general English usage, it is likely that there are some texts included in them that represent the discourse of such speakers. The second reason why we may find items at N-1 and N+1 that deviate from the overall patterns in semantic prosody that we have identified is because the negative element might be expressed elsewhere in the sentence or utterance. While some of the instances above suggest a positive semantic prosody at first, a closer inspection of the extended co-text reveals some rather negative connotations. For example, *genetic endowment* is used in relation to something 'inaccessible', as shown in the following example taken from the *BNC*:

> ECN 500 Considerable differences have arisen between those who have tried to show that aggression is a ';natural'; human attribute, having its origins in **genetic endowment**, or something equally inaccessible to self-intervention and control.

Genetic richness is used in relation to the process of genetic engineering, which in turn depletes genetic richness as shown in the following example:

> AB6 453 And at that point, of course, it swings into the issue of bio-diversity and the threat that destruction of the tropical rainforests, with their **genetic richness**, will mean more and more plants being lost for good.

Similarly, we can find a negative semantic prosody in the vicinity of the other examples on this list, which underlines the importance of studying an extended concordance output in order to determine the semantic prosody.

Concluding remarks

How does the analysis of the lemma GENE contribute to our understanding of ideology? The spoken data we have examined has produced a very limited sample of concordance lines and it is therefore difficult to make generalizations on the basis of this data. However, it has shown a tendency for a negative semantic prosody in contexts in the corpus where people are most off-guard, and a more neutral prosody in the pedagogic genre. In the analysis of the large-scale corpora, that include mainly written data, we have uncovered evidence of negative semantic prosodies, especially in constructions where a process of genetic alteration is concerned.

The findings thus illustrate an ambivalence towards genetic biotechnology, with a notable tendency towards a negative conceptualization of the issues that underlie this debate. A more detailed analysis of the different sources of the texts in the written corpus would allow for more fine-grained distinctions between the opponents and proponents of biotechnology, but the overwhelming evidence of negative semantic prosody in this context is striking.

As most of the data for this study come from the 1980s and 1990s we can only provide a synchronic snapshot of how the lemma GENE was used at a time when genetic breakthroughs revolutionized our understanding of life and of the meaning of life. It would be interesting to analyse the diachronic changes in the uses and meanings of *gene* over time, from the 1960s, when genetic science had its first scientific and popular peak to the 1990s, when it had its second.

Summary

This chapter has offered a brief introduction to the study of ideology with the use of corpus resources. It has outlined the various angles from which particular ideologies can be studied and their relationship to different corpus resources. The focus of this chapter has been on the discussion of the study of semantic prosodies as an approach to uncovering attitudes that relate to particular lexical items. The sample analysis has illustrated such an approach with reference to the lemma GENE, and has highlighted differences in prosody in terms of the different variants of this lemma and the associated discourse in which they occur. This chapter has shown that corpus-based analyses of individual lexical items and phrases, that have been identified as relevant references in the study of particular aspects of ideology, can be useful in providing evidence from different domains of discourse and from different discourse communities. However, the process of identifying such items and the ideology that drives such a choice will need further discussion in future studies that are concerned with the issues outlined in this chapter.

Activities

1. Public perceptions of risk are a major issue for policy makers and for politicians. This is one of the reasons why research in this area has flurried over the past decade. Beck (1992: 226) points out that, 'To the same degree as sensitivity to risks grows in the public, a political need for minimization research arises'. However, what do we mean by sensitivity to risk and how can we assess what kind of meaning the public assigns to this notion? When we consider the literature on risk we find that a number of claims are being made without much empirical support. Consider, for example, a passage from *Risk* by Deborah Lupton (1999: 8–9):

    > In everyday lay people's language, risk tends to be used to refer to almost exclusively to a threat, hazard, danger or harm: we 'risk our life savings' by investing on the stock exchange, or 'put our marriage at risk' by having an affair. The term is also used more weakly to refer to a somewhat negative rather than disastrous outcome, as in the phrase 'If you go outside in this rain, you'll risk catching a cold.' In this usage, risk means somewhat less than a possible danger or a threat, more an unfortunate or annoying event. Risk is therefore a very loose term in everyday parlance. Issues of calculable probability are not necessarily important to the colloquial use of risk. Risk and uncertainty tend to be treated as conceptually the same thing: for example, the term 'risk' is often used to denote a phenomenon that has the potential to deliver substantial harm, whether or not the probability of this harm eventuating is estimable.

    From the claim above it follows that there is a difference between the 'expert' conceptualization of risk, which is associated with calculable probability, and the public's conceptualization of risk, which is related to uncertainty. The following concordance lines have been taken from the socio-cultural category in the CANCODE corpus, i.e. from a one million word sub-section of casual conversation. Consider this concordance output in light of the quote by Lupton above and discuss any patterns in the concordance data that suggest a deviation from her claims:

It's a	**risk**	that you've got no choice in really
And the	**risk**	is higher
Still it's worth the	**risk**	eh.
I think it's a big	**risk**	or or or
a big	**risk**	a small
know if there's a dangerous	**risk**	maybe they should relocate.
You realize it's a major	**risk**.	
was just wondering how much	**risk**	these people were er on a lesser
that's the kind of possible	**risk?**	

+I'd try and minimize the	**risk**	as much as possible of an accident
Well there's less	**risk**	to less people isn't there.
promise and say there's a low	**risk**	or it was very unlikely.
you feel if that was the	**risk?**	
your rocks off without the	**risk**	of getting arrested for murder
You're in a high	**risk**	area.
person knew there was a	**risk**	with it.
But you've got the existing	**risk**.	
You'd know the existing	**risk**	so you'd be putting more people at
to make industry reduce the	**risk**	to the public.
because it increases your	**risk**	of having an asthma attack.
I mean like that's a	**risk**	isn't it.
and there was a s= a slight	**risk**	then I don't think

Can you find a semantic preference and/or prosody for the word *risk* as it is used in this random list of concordance lines? What are they and how do they relate to Lupton's claims?[6]

2. One of the aims of critical discourse analysis outlined above is to make explicit those instances where language is used to reinforce inequality and dominance. Run a concordance search of the lexical item *old* using the BNC online simple search interface and in the Collins Wordbanks*Online* corpus and make a note of any instances that relate to human beings. Then make a note of those instances where *old* is used with reference to males and to females and compare the terms that are used to describe them. What does this exploration tell you about the representation of men and women with regard to age? Is there a difference in semantic preference or prosody? And how do your results relate to the origin of the corpus data?

Further reading

Using a corpus-based approach Stubbs (1996) shows how different ideological stances in school books on physical and human geography can be analysed via a study of causativity and modality. O'Halloran and Coffin (2004) illustrate how corpus-based techniques can be helpful in analysing how readers relate to particular points of views presented to them in different texts. Charteris-Black (2004) deals with the issue of how metaphors can be critically analysed with the use of corpus approaches. Fairclough (2000) provides an in depth analysis of the discourse of the British New Labour party by comparing the language used in documents that relate to the 'Old' Labour party with those that relate to New Labour. The comparison is carried out on the basis of various corpora specifically developed for this purpose. Baker (2005) offers a comprehensive corpus-based study of the way in which public discourses construct the image of gay men. Teubert (2000) gives a corpus-based account of Euroscepticism in Britain which draws on a corpus of online documents.

Notes

1. Part of this analysis is based on Adolphs *et al.* (2003).
2. See chapter two for further information about the different corpora.
3. See McCarthy (1998) for a comprehensive description of the different categories.
4. It is important to highlight that the instances summarized in this table were drawn from a range of different conversations in the respective categories.
5. These results were generated in the year 2002 via the Cobuild online collocation sampler. All results are based on t-score analyses.
6. I am grateful to Brigitte Nerlich and Craig Hamilton for allowing me to use this examle, which is taken from a co-written manuscript that is currently being prepared for publication.

7 Language teaching applications

Introduction

Electronic text analysis has had a considerable effect on the area of language teaching and a number of the large corpora funded by publishing houses were built with the aim of facilitating corpus-based lexicography to inform English language teaching dictionaries and grammars. These include, amongst others, the *Longman Dictionary of Contemporary English*, the *Cambridge Advanced Learner's Dictionary*, the *Collins COBUILD Learner's Dictionary* and the *Macmillan English Dictionary*. Similarly, new grammars of English have been designed based on corpus evidence, such as the *Longman Grammar of Spoken and Written English* for example.

The motivation for using a corpus approach in this area is related partly to the attraction of being able to offer a description of actual language in use, and thus to capture contextual properties in relation to linguistic forms, and partly because the study of authentic texts has revealed some inconsistencies between the use of lexical items and grammatical structures in corpora, and those found in traditional language textbooks that are based purely on introspective judgements. In addition, as discussed in previous chapters, some of the properties of individual words and phrases that become visible through corpus analysis, such as frequencies and collocations for example, are not generally open to intuition, which means that corpus analysis can help inform the syllabus design process. As Ellis (1997: 129) argues, 'speaking natively is speaking idiomatically using frequent and familiar collocations, and the job of the language learner is to learn these familiar word sequences'. At the same time, corpus explorations can be carried out by learners themselves and can be used as an integral part of the learning process. This chapter explores the use of electronic text analysis in the area of English Language Teaching (ELT).

The chapter is split into three sections that broadly reflect the different areas in which electronic text analysis has influenced ELT theory and practice. It starts with an overview of how insights generated through methods of electronic text analysis in the area of language description might affect the overall priorities of what is being taught in the language classroom. The section following this discussion deals with the way in which such insights might directly inform the design of teaching materials. The use of corpus data for ELT purposes has been at the centre of an on-going debate amongst corpus linguists and ELT practitioners and a brief overview of the key arguments will be presented as part of this section. In the following section, we turn our attention to the learner and explore the extent to which, given a corpus resource and suitable software, language learners themselves might turn into researchers and facilitate their own learning process through guided corpus tasks.

The electronic text resources that lie at the heart of the types of ELT applications discussed in this chapter tend to consist of spoken and written English produced by native speakers of this language. However, there is now a growing interest in the study of learner English and in the development of corpora of this variety (for examples of learner corpora see chapter two). This is partly because such resources can be helpful in analysing patterns of deviation from native speaker English and, as such, highlight particular problem areas for learners. Furthermore, interest in learner English has also grown because of the substantial scope for describing emerging varieties of non-native speaker English in a world where a growing percentage of discourse in English is used between non-native speakers. The final section of this chapter will thus provide a brief overview of some of the research in this area.

Electronic text resources for language teaching and learning

While there is now widespread access, albeit mainly on a sample basis, to some of the major corpus resources discussed in chapter two, the question of what kind of corpus is appropriate for the use by learners and teachers extends beyond considerations of access. The texts that are contained in any of these corpora become a key issue in the ELT context, while considerations about representativeness and balance are maybe less pressing. When it comes to the use of corpus resources in the ELT context the following issues have to be taken into account:

- What is the role of the corpus? Is it to be used by teachers, students or syllabus designers? If it is used by students, are all texts at a level which suits the students' level of proficiency?
- What is the particular learning objective? Is the corpus used in the context of grammar or vocabulary teaching? If it is the latter, then the corpus needs to be of considerable size in order to provide a sufficient number of instances of an individual item.
- What is the particular genre that is being explored? Is the corpus used to inform teaching and learning in English for Academic Purposes, or in Spoken Discourse for example? Corpus analysis of different genres has highlighted key differences in linguistic choices, and this observation allows researchers,

teachers and syllabus designers to tailor their teaching material towards the aims and needs of a diverse range of learners. Hyland (2003), for example, discusses the various steps involved in teaching writing to language learners, taking into account the constraints of the particular genre. In developing corpus resources for language teaching purposes the target genre has to be given due consideration in the process.

Some of these issues overlap and together they become the basis for the design criteria of a corpus that is suitable for specific needs in the ELT context. It should be noted that the resource does not necessarily need to be substantial to be of value for ELT purposes, and smaller corpora can often easily be assembled from scratch. Tribble (1997) shows how small corpora of under one million words can be of considerable benefit in the ELT context. The applications he discusses span a whole range of areas, including high frequency lexis in a specific domain, collocation, colligation and semantic prosody, grammar and discourse, as well as contrastive analyses of lexical items in different domains.

Language description and ELT pedagogy

Over the last three decades ELT pedagogy has been marked by the Communicative Language Teaching (CLT) approach, which focuses on the development of skills that allow the learner to actively use a language in a given context. This model is particularly concerned with the teaching of how language realizes particular functions in discourse. The model stands in contrast to other approaches, which have often concentrated on the teaching of various aspects of the language system in isolation, such as vocabulary and grammar for example. The emphasis of the latter tends to be on fostering accurate productive and receptive knowledge in the language acquisition process. However, as Carter (1998: 51) points out, 'In spite of numerous pedagogic advantages, communicative teaching has not encouraged in students habits of observation, noticing, or conscious exploration of grammatical forms and function'.

The impact of corpus linguistics in the area of language description has led to the question of whether a corpus might be a suitable resource to provide the basis for this type of exploration by the student, since the data not only presents us with new information about language patterns in use, but, at the same time, provides the communicative background to the types of discourses in which such patterns occur. We will return in more detail to the way in which electronic text analysis might inform language teaching material design later on in this chapter. For now we will have a closer look at the role of electronic text resources as a basis for language description in the ELT context.

Until quite recently, language teaching materials were based almost exclusively on made-up examples. However, as we have seen in chapters three and four, the analysis of large corpora of electronic texts provides additional evidence about a language that would not otherwise be accessible through intuition, such as information about collocations and frequency for example. Both of these language properties are particularly important in the ELT context and will be further discussed below.

Word frequency

Word frequency information can be used to design syllabuses based on the needs of particular learners with regard to both the sequence of the vocabulary items that are being taught and the overall size of the vocabulary store that is required to achieve an adequate coverage of a language. In a study of the language of Australian workers, Schonell *et al.* (1956) found that 2000 word families covered nearly 99 per cent of the words used in their speech overall. Word families include all derivations and inflections of a particular lexical stem. The results of this study, which was based on a corpus of just over half a million words, reflect the particular distribution of words in a language as described by Zipf (1935). As such, we can expect a relatively small number of very high frequency words to account for a large percentage of the language. This is borne out by more recent corpus evidence (Adolphs and Schmitt 2003), and has implications for making judgements about how many word families a learner needs to know in order to be able to engage in a particular language (Coxhead 2000). Further research has shown that there are differences in vocabulary coverage depending on the particular context of language use. Adolphs and Schmitt (2004), for example, show that the level of coverage for a given number of words is higher in corpora of transactional encounters, such as exchanges between customers and sales assistants, compared with corpora of more interactional encounters, such as conversations between friends. This means that learners require a larger vocabulary store to interact at a social level than to engage in a service encounter, which is maybe not surprising given the large range of topics that tend to be covered in informal interactions between friends compared with the relatively rigid format of service encounters.

While this kind of information derived from corpora provides learners with a list of words that make up the core of the language, and that might therefore be useful to know, there are a number of issues with this type of list. Firstly, an automated frequency count of individual words cannot distinguish between different meanings of polysemous words. While there tends to be a dominant meaning in terms of frequency, there is still a need to distinguish between the different senses of individual words and to make a judgement about the amount of time devoted to less frequent senses in the teaching context. At a practical level, the frequency of individual words might be distorted because of their polysemous properties. Take the word *see* for example, which is amongst the 100 most frequent words in the *CANCODE* corpus, with an overall frequency of 11,922. The meanings of *see* in the

corpus include *visit, notice, attend to* and *understand*, as shown in the following concordance lines:

get them done in Boots you	**see**.	
Oh I	**see**	yeah.
Once my granddad came to	**see**	me.
go over when you	**see**	asbestos.
he just slid underneath you	**see**.	
We're coming up to	**see**	your wood later on+
nine o'clock I wanna go and	**see**	Doreen.
I'll I'll	**see**	to you.

Apart from these practical considerations, Bogaards and Laufer (2004: x) point out
that 'a crucial factor in L2 vocabulary acquisition, regardless of word frequency, is
word "learnability"'. The ease with which an individual word can be learned
depends on a range of factors, including interference with the learner's first language. There may thus be a case for re-arranging frequency lists according to particular teaching purposes in order to account for such factors. This is a classic example of the tension between results generated through electronic text analysis and
their translation into teaching materials, which has been a core issue in this debate.

Finally, the use of frequency lists in the context of syllabus design poses the
problem of decontextualization. While it is possible to generate frequency lists
from specific corpora that are deemed to be relevant to a particular group of learners, such as corpora of academic writing for example, the frequency lists themselves do not provide patterns of usage in relation to the discourse context and co-
text. In the context of a Communicative Language Teaching (CLT) approach, both
the discourse context and the co-text are particularly important in establishing the
communicative background to language use. The discourse context provides the
backdrop against which the appropriateness of a particular utterance or sentence
is judged, while the immediate co-text reveals information about the phraseology
that surrounds a particular word and contributes to its functional interpretation.
The teaching of individual functional phrases has been at the heart of the CLT
approach but a lot of the material in this area has been based on invented examples. The analysis of collections of naturally occurring data in this context allows
us to derive actual phrases and relate them to particular types of discourse, as will
be illustrated in the next section.

Phraseology

In chapters three and four, various ways of calculating the attraction of individual
words in an electronic text resource were discussed. Such calculation aids the
identification of multi-word units, which are pervasive in language use. In the context of CLT, the multi-word units that are used to introduce individual language
functions are a key focus and discussed in many traditional ELT textbooks. The

appropriate use of such multi-word units is an important skill in the successful mastery of a second language (Nattinger and DeCarrico 1992).

There are a number of language textbooks and grammars including some that draw on corpus data, which offer lists of 'functional synonyms', such as the ones below taken from Leech and Svartvik (1994: 168). These introduce various ways of realizing the communicative function of making suggestions:

Suggestions:
I suggest they take the night train.
You can read these two chapters before tomorrow (if you like).
You could be cleaning the office while I'm away.
You might have a look at this book.
Why don't you call on me tomorrow.

Could and Might indicate tentative suggestions.

Suggestions involving the speaker:
I suggest we go to bed early, and make an early start tomorrow.
Shall we listen to some music?
Let's not waste time.
Why don't we have a party?
How about a game of cards?
What about having a drink?'

While an overview of the phrases above can be useful in a pedagogic context, in that they offer a range of options for the realization of a particular speech act, the analysis of corpus data can add additional information about the use of these phrases that is of value to both students and teachers. Firstly, it allows a closer analysis of possible phrases surrounding each individual grammatical construction and speech act verb. Secondly, a corpus analysis of such items provides information about the frequency of different phrases in relation to their context of use, thus favouring the issue of *appropriate use in context* over perceived levels of politeness. If we take the example of the direct speech act verb *suggest*, a search of this realization in the *CANCODE* corpus shows the different types of phrases that emerge, as well as differences in distribution according to discourse context.

Overall the speech act verb *suggest* occurs 169 times in the corpus. Once we take out those instances where a suggestion is reported and where it introduces an idea rather than a direct action (as in 'this suggests to me that...') and count only those examples where *suggest* marks a proposal for a specific line of action, 102 instances remain. In terms of discourse context, the majority of these instances occur in more formal contexts so we find a combined figure of 75 instances in the professional encounters and in service encounters, while the remainder occurs in conversations between friends and family.

In terms of the phraseology that surrounds this speech act verb, a simple examination of the sorted concordance output can be used as a first step. It soon becomes clear that the verb *suggest* tends to be highly modalized, which in turn establishes the types of phrases that we are likely to encounter. An analysis of the 10 most frequent collocates using *Wordsmith Tools* is shown in table 7.1.

We can see here that *suggest that* is one of the strongest patterns to the right of the search word, while *would* is the most frequent collocate to the left. Other modal items that occur in the position directly preceding the word *suggest*, but that are not on this list as they are not amongst the 10 most frequent collocates, are *gonna* (5) and *could* (2), while the modality markers *perhaps* (7) and *should* (5) occur in the position directly following the word *suggest*.

An analysis of clusters using *Wordsmith Tools* generates the following list for the 10 most frequent 3-word recurrent sequences:

	Cluster	Frequency
1	I would suggest	23
2	to suggest that	19
3	suggest that you	13
4	would suggest that	10
5	suggest that the	8
6	I suggest we	7
7	I suggest you	6
8	I suggest that	5
9	suggest you do	5
10	like to suggest	4

Table 7.1 Ten most frequent collocates of the word *suggest* in the CANCODE corpus.

Word	Fifth word left	Fourth word left	Third word left	Second word left	First word left	NODE	First word right	Second word right	Third word right	Fourth word right	Fifth word right
SUGGEST	0	0	0	0	1	169	0	0	0	0	0
THAT	1	2	4	2	2	0	65	11	4	4	3
YOU	7	2	5	3	10	0	12	22	8	7	3
THE	4	8	4	1	0	0	4	11	7	11	7
WOULD	1	2	1	2	26	0	0	0	1	0	0
YEAH	4	7	4	2	1	0	0	2	3	2	1
AND	1	4	6	3	2	0	1	1	1	2	4
WHAT	2	3	9	7	0	0	1	0	1	1	1

While there is bound to be a certain amount of overlap between these individual clusters (i.e. the cluster *I would suggest* may include instances of the cluster *suggest that you* for example), an examination of the concordance output, together with a collocation search and a cluster search, allows us to make some observations about the phraseology of the verb *suggest*. The following concordance output from CANCODE mirrors the overall patterns found in the data discussed above:

What I'd	**suggest**	that you do is to arrange a time to come in and
So what I'd like to	**suggest**	at the moment is if anyone has any matters
certain date then I would	**suggest**	you just give us a call a couple of days
Now I would	**suggest**	that you run the two accounts alongside
I think it's feasible to	**suggest**	that perhaps you should view the
What I was gonna	**suggest**	to you is to have a go at one

These patterns can be easily gleaned from the concordance output, even without the additional calculation of collocates and clusters. The phraseology of the verb *suggest* includes not only a tendency towards modalization but also towards the grammatical structure of pseudo-cleft constructions (e.g. 'What I'd suggest that you do'), which is a further device for a speaker to distance themselves from a proposition. The verb *suggest* is thus highly direct when used outside of a downtoning structure and its preferred use is as part of a phrase which includes some form of modalization. This type of observation is, of course, highly relevant to the learner as it provides him or her with a choice of constructions that are appropriate in a particular context. Further information about the different contexts in which the different constructions occur can also be gathered from the corpus and included in the list of patterns.

The analysis of phrases based on electronic texts is not only useful because it can generate lists of units that might be appropriate in particular contexts, but also because the acquisition of such phrases can aid second language speech fluency. As such phrases are stored and recalled as single entities in the mind, their use leads to more fluent speech production, which has been demonstrated in samples of learner English (Wood 2004). This again highlights the potential of corpus-based descriptions for the ELT context.

Other features of naturally occurring language

The exploration of collections of naturally occurring spoken and written language has led to a wide range of further observations about language in use. The analysis of spoken English in particular has shown that there are certain patterns and regularities in the relatively messy nature of spoken interaction. These include particular instances of spoken grammar, such as the types of pseudo-cleft constructions listed above, new word formations (such as those that end on the suffix -ish, as in 'let's meet at six-ish') and a wealth of other creative adaptations of vocabulary and grammar.[1] Traditional ELT textbooks have not tended to take such observations into account and have opted, instead, for data that is based on the much tidier, written model, even in units that deal with conversational exchanges. There may be good pedagogic reasons for this, some of which will be discussed in the next section. However, corpus research shows that a number of these linguistic choices are made to establish and maintain social relationships between speakers and thus to foster interpersonal rapport (see, for example, Carter 2004). One of the key questions, therefore, is whether or not learners should be provided with the opportunity of engaging with examples of the type of discourse pattern featured in the extract below, which is taken from a conversation between friends recorded in the *CANCODE* corpus:

> <S 02> Well why did you say you can make the red stand out if there isn't any red? It's blue green red and yellow isn't it.
> <S 01> Well it's a kind of orangey red isn't it.
> <S 03> Yeah.
> <S 04> Or is it a reddy orange?
> <S 02> It's not a reddy orange.
> <S 01> Orangey red.
> <S 03> Or reddish.
> <S 02> No. It's orangey red not reddy orange.
> <S 03> That's good.
> <S 03> Yeah.

The extract shows a number of new word formations that are used in a creative way and in a context where the process of negotiating a particular colour appears to be just as important as creating an atmosphere of convergence between the speakers. The relevance of this type of information in the ELT context will be briefly discussed in the next section.

Corpus-informed material design

As we have seen in the last section, new insights gained through the analysis of electronic text collections with regard to language description have considerable potential for the ELT context. However, the past decade has seen a heated debate over the transferability of the insights gained through corpus analysis into the ELT classroom. This section will first consider an example of corpus-based material design and then introduce some of the key arguments in the on-going debate about the use of such materials in the ELT context.

Examples of how corpus data can be used in the context of material design range from the use of texts and concordance lines that have been pre-selected by the teacher, either for illustration of particular patterns or as the basis for gap filling tasks, to guided explorations of raw corpus-data by the student. The use of concordance data can be particularly valuable in the illustration of different meanings of semantically similar lexical items. Take, for example, the verbs *see* and *watch*, which may cause difficulty in use for students whose first language does not have the same correlates. A study of the selected concordance lines below, taken from the *CANCODE* corpus, allows the student to generate rules for the appropriate use of the respective items:

See:

go over when you	**see**	asbestos.
I can't	**see**	what's on me plate.
We're coming up to	**see**	your wood later on+
have a right to actually	**see**	the the directors' account numbers.
remember the last time I did	**see**	him.
he small bowel where you can	**see**	overlapping structures make er er in
in some areas people will	**see**	this screen and it will be the only
You	**see**	lots of the uniforms.
coach rides because em we	**see**	all the houses and the people close
the station and back just to	**see**	the old side.
Obviously you don't get to	**see**	the report that Ikea base this on but
motorway and so they could	**see**	the size of the carbines.
I could	**see**	her golden nose ring and earrings.

Watch:

the meal especially to	**watch**	it.
then we would hope to go	**watch**	some Hindi films there.
We could stay and	**watch**	a video if I can find a video to
Go up and	**watch**	your telly.
Oh you	**watch**	the travel programmes don't you.
+to	**watch**	people eating it and all.
call it off a bit you know	**watch**	what they were putting in.
I sort of stand back and	**watch**	my kids sort of+
colosseum and they used to	**watch**	all these gladiators fighting.
And we stay in the dunes	**watch**	the sunrise go back up to the house
wave off stop a while and	**watch**	us two guys track off just as
out for picnics and er er	**watch**	her painting on these excursions.
And I says "They	**watch**	me do things and they do so-and-so

The concordance data above has been selected to illustrate the difference between *see* and *watch* in those instances where they relate to the physical process of using one's vision. Here, *see* is used predominantly to express the meaning of 'noticing', in relation to an inanimate object, while *watch* is mainly used in relation to an intended process of focusing on something that is animate, and often occurs over a period of time. Subsequent analyses of the other meaning senses of both items, as well as their use as part of multi-word units (*watch out, I see what you mean, etc*), might complete a discussion of these two words. The knowledge of both items thus acquired can then be tested via fill-the-gap exercises, possibly based on a different set of concordance lines.[2]

While the value of the use of corpus examples as part of the material design process is obvious to some, there are a number of interrelated issues attached to this approach that have led to some debate in this area. These issues will be discussed briefly below:

- **The discrepancies between observed language in use and invented examples of language data for materials design**. There are now a substantial number of studies that highlight the considerable differences between the language we find in textbooks and the language we find in text corpora (see for example Gilmore 2004). Invented dialogues and multi-party conversations in textbooks are particularly contrived and the common features of naturally occurring interaction, such as ellipsis, turn overlaps, false starts and repetition, are often missing from the textbook data. Similarly, vague language is a particular feature of unplanned discourse which is not generally found in classroom discourse (Fox 1998).

  Sinclair and Renouf (1988) discuss the prevalence of delexicalized verbs, such as *make* and *take*, in a corpus, and highlight the lack of discussion of such functions in EFL textbooks. As outlined in chapter four, one of the main discoveries to come out of the large-scale study of electronic texts is the interrelationship between lexis and grammar. This insight indicates that, in the ELT context, syntactic and grammatical structures should not be taught in isolation from vocabulary items (see Sinclair and Renouf 1988 for a discussion), but that we should, instead, be looking to the development of a corpus-driven lexical syllabus in order to reflect the reality of language in use (Willis 1990, 2003).

- **The tension between pedagogical needs in the ELT classroom and corpus evidence**. The question of whether it is desirable for language learning tasks to reflect naturally occurring language use has been raised repeatedly (see Widdowson 1998). Language learning tasks are designed to promote particular skills in a specific sequence, which are carefully brought together to reflect a given stage of the learning process. Invented dialogues used in textbooks might focus on the acquisition of a specific set of vocabulary, grammatical constructions or speech acts. And it could be argued that the added features of naturally occurring dialogues, such as ellipsis and false starts, for example, might distract from the set learning outcomes. Similarly, we may find that certain naturally occurring dialogues present the learner with vocabulary and grammar that is too advanced for their particular level, where invented conversations would allow the materials designers to control the level of vocabulary and grammar knowledge that is required to follow the interaction. On the other hand, it could be argued that every learner should be given the opportunity to engage with the type of language that they are likely to encounter when they are operating outside of the classroom in an L2, and that we should therefore expose learners to naturally occurring language data wherever possible. One way of addressing this issue would be to pre-edit corpus data to fit the needs of a particular group of students. However, this would change the nature of the data and run counter to the objective of exposure to naturally occurring language in use.

- **The status of corpus data as samples of 'authentic' language**. This issue is closely related to the last one and centres around the notion of authenticity. It is often argued that students should be exposed to authentic samples of language either to facilitate awareness of language in use or to teach particular features of such language samples explicitly. Authenticity refers here to the status of the texts as forms of discourse which have been produced independent of the learning task, in an authentic context, for a particular audience (which tends to be different to that of the language learner). However, some argue that the notion of authenticity relates to the relationship between a particular piece of discourse and the response that it triggers in its immediate audience (see Widdowson 1998 for a discussion). This would imply that once texts are taken out of their immediate context, stored in large electronic databases, and reproduced for the teaching context, they are taken out of their authentic environment. The learner, then, has to process such texts with reference to a different context than the one in which they originated, a context which may not reflect his or her communicative goals in the classroom context. On the other hand, naturally occurring data can be contextualized for the learner and the use of such data in the classroom, therefore, not only allows for an integration of some discussion of cultural background to the data, but also empowers the learner by giving him or her the opportunity to engage with genuine language in use (see Carter 1998).

- **The model of the 'native speaker' in the classroom**. This issue is again closely related to the preceding ones in that it relates to the nature of the data that we might wish to include in language teaching material. Recent research has shown that language learners regard the approximation to native speaker English as a main goal in the language learning process (Timmis 2002). This observation has prompted further exploration of two questions in this debate. Firstly, what do we mean by 'native speaker', and secondly, what is the value of the native speaker model in the ELT context. While the notion of the 'native speaker' of English tends to be used to refer to those speakers whose first language is English, this notion is far from unified and remains largely unanalysed (Pennycook 1994). The vast number of different varieties of 'native speaker' English means that this notion cannot easily be translated into one particular standard for the language classroom. The choice of a particular variety of

English for the ELT context, even down to fine-grained choices of regional or local variety, becomes a highly political issue. This is, of course, not merely an issue that relates to naturally occurring data but also to invented examples. At the same time, the proportion of English discourse exchanged between non-native speakers is growing rapidly, with an overall increase in globalization and internationalization (Crystal 1997). This raises the question whether native speaker models are the most appropriate basis for language learners, who may predominantly use their L2 to operate in an international, rather than a 'native', context.

Despite the overall debate over the use of naturally occurring language samples in the context of ELT materials, substantial progress has been made in the area of corpus-informed lexicography for English as a Foreign Language (EFL) purposes as highlighted at the beginning of this chapter. Many dictionaries and grammar reference books today draw on corpus data in some way or another (Biber *et al*. 1999, Carter and McCarthy 2006). However, the integration of naturally occurring language samples into EFL course books has been less prominent, partly because of the reasons outlined above. Yet, there has been a steady increase in the exploitation of corpus data and corpus methods in the modern EFL classrooms, which will be the focus of the next section.

Data-driven learning

The approach of data-driven learning has been developed for use in the ELT classroom (Johns 1991). It is akin to the idea of consciousness raising (Ellis 1993) in the way that it allows the learner to explore language data and thus to derive patterns of language use. This approach turns the language learner into the language researcher, giving him or her more autonomy, and by doing so increasing learner motivation. At the same time, letting the learner explore corpus data helps them develop crucial skills of hypothesis testing and data analysis.

Depending on the level of the learner, there are various approaches that can be taken to facilitate the process of data-driven learning. These range from very controlled learning tasks, where the teacher may select a few specific concordance lines that illustrate a grammatical point or usage of a particular lexical item, to more complex tasks for advanced learners. The latter might consist of a task where the learners are asked to consult raw corpus data in order to determine the use and associated patterns of a set of lexical or grammatical items, or it might involve the learner setting up their own line of linguistic enquiry and using raw corpus data to address this task. The different stages are thus tightly linked to the involvement of the teacher in the planning stage of the activity and, as such, require a good deal of judgement and sensitivity with regard to the level of the learner, the corpus data and the benefit which may be derived from the activity.

The use of electronic text resources has more recently also been introduced in teaching contexts outside the ELT classroom. Küebler (2004) reports on an experiment in which she uses the *WebCorp* interface, together with finite corpora, as the basis for teaching students an approach to machine translation. Furthermore, Kettemann (1995) shows how the analysis of literary corpora can be used in the teaching of literature. Overall, then, there seems to be a growing awareness of the scope of using corpus data in fostering the types of analytical skills that are facilitated by the processes outlined above.

Electronic text analysis and learner English

There has been a growing interest in the electronic exploration of learner corpora since the late 1980s (Granger 1998, Granger *et al.* 2002). This line of research has led to the development of powerful resources of learner language and has facilitated descriptions of emerging patterns found in different varieties of learner English.[3]

At the most basic level, there are three ways of approaching learner corpora. We can analyse any patterns that emerge via the application of the kinds of corpus-linguistic methods that have been discussed in this volume. This process leads to better descriptions of learner language, just as it has led to better descriptions of the language collected in native speaker corpora. We may also wish to analyse learner corpora in a contrastive way with native speaker corpora, with the aim of highlighting potential differences and overlaps. This approach allows us to determine the level of the learner at any one time in terms of the approximation of their language use to that of native speakers. It also helps us determine areas where students overuse or under-use particular constructions or lexical items. The process of comparing learner corpora to some native speaker norm has led to the development of elaborate annotation schemes that tag learner errors. The Universite Catholique de Leuven Error Editor (UCLEE) for example distinguishes between different types of errors and allows for a manual annotation of learner texts (Granger 2002). A subsequent search of individual types of tags can then show patterns of particular errors. It should be noted that the term 'error' in this context has caused some debate in the field, as it implies that we assign the status of 'correctness' to native speaker English. As discussed above, the status of the native speaker is related to the notion of ownership of the language, however, with the increasing use of English as a lingua franca, it becomes problematic to assign ownership and related judgements with regard to 'correct' usage.

The third way of approaching learner corpora is through longitudinal research. While the majority of studies in second language acquisition are time-limited snapshots of learner performance, this type of research is concerned with the development of learner English either with reference to native speaker corpora or as an investigation of language development in its own right.

All of these three types of analysis can have implications for second language acquisition research and for language teaching. In particular comparisons with native speaker corpora can highlight patterns of deviations that can be strategically integrated into classroom teaching.

An example of the latter approach could include the analysis of multi-word units in learner English over time.[4] We have already mentioned the importance of multi-word units and phrases for learners of English earlier in the chapter. In order to analyse the development of use of such units I have chosen to compare the spoken discourse produced by a Chinese learner of English in two interviews. The first interview, which was an informal discussion about life in England, was held immediately after the student arrived in the UK, while the last interview was held seven months after her arrival. The interviews are part of the Nottingham International Corpus (NIC), which currently includes just under half a million words of international spoken English, collected through semi-structured interviews. Table 7.2 shows the ten most frequent 3-word sequences used by the language learner in the first and the last interview, as well as a list of the most frequent 3-word sequences in the *CANCODE* corpus.

We can see from this data that there is a change in the types of sequences used in interview 1 and interview 2. In interview 1 half of the sequences used are markers of hesitation and disfluency, while in the second interview these have been substituted with sequences that have a clear lexical core and thus add to the fluency of the discourse. While there is probably some overlap between *it's very nice* and *so it's very* in the second interview, we can see that the hesitation markers from the first interview have made way for more evaluative language, which, in itself, is an interesting observation in terms of learner language development.

Table 7.2 Ten most frequent three-word sequences in interview 1 and interview 2, and in the CANCODE corpus.

Interview 1	Freq.	%	Interview 2	Freq.	%	CANCODE	Freq.	%
I want to	20	0.36	a lot of	33	0.85	I don't know	5,274	0.11
just er I	17	0.31	it's very nice	23	0.59	a lot of	2,851	0.06
I think so	15	0.27	so it's very	15	0.38	I mean I	2,186	0.05
and I think	12	0.22	so it's nice	14	0.36	I don't think	2,142	0.04
I I I	12	0.22	lot of things	12	0.31	do you think	1,503	0.03
yeah just er	12	0.22	I got very	9	0.23	do you want	1,417	0.03
you must er	12	0.22	got a lot	8	0.21	one of the	1,311	0.03
I think this	11	0.20	join the lecture	8	0.21	you have to	1,297	0.03
um just er	11	0.20	the lecture and	8	0.21	it was a	1,271	0.03
a lot of	9	0.16	I got some	7	0.18	you know I	1,231	0.03

When we compare this data with the native speaker corpus, we notice a relatively small degree of overlap (*a lot of* is the only overlapping sequence). Interestingly, the majority of the most frequent sequences in the native speaker corpus are concerned with the presentation and elicitation of opinions and knowledge, and as such they are highly interactive in nature. This type of interactive format can be difficult for the learner to achieve, as it does not resemble the kind of discourse that the learner is traditionally exposed to in the form of ELT materials.

Frequency lists of recurrent sequences and individual words in learner output can therefore be used to track the development of the learner. A frequency list based on a corpus of student writing can show whether a particular vocabulary item previously taught is being used by the student(s). The comparison of such lists with a list derived from native speaker corpora of written English can illustrate the approximation to native speaker proficiency.

The example above is a basic illustration of some of the potential investigations that can be carried out with the help of learner corpora. The data used here is limited in range and quantity and the resulting sequences are therefore not very robust in terms of possible generalizations that may be drawn on the basis of this data. However, the scope of the use of learner corpora is substantial and new applications are being continually developed.

Summary

This chapter has dealt with a number of issues that relate to the use of electronic text analysis in the ELT context. The three main areas that have been discussed are the implications of corpus analysis for syllabus design, material development and data-driven learning. In addition, this chapter has introduced the study of learner English and its relevance to language description, pedagogy and second language acquisition research. The sample analyses carried out in this chapter have highlighted the potential of this approach in the ELT context, both from a student's and from a teacher's perspective.

This chapter has also outlined some of the challenges and questions that arise in relation to the use of corpus data and corpus-based research for pedagogic purposes. These relate to the nature of the data and whether any particular variety of English should be accepted as a preferred norm in the ELT context, and also to the nature of the transfer of corpus data into the classroom.

More research is needed in this area before these issues can be addressed with some confidence. The study of different varieties of English, including those that emerge through interactions between non-native speakers, might add to this discussion in that it will encourage debates about language norms while at the same time highlighting the fact that ELT practice has to take account of the aspirations and expectations of the individual language learner. These expectations and aspirations are likely to relate to the particular discourse contexts that the learner has identified as the core areas in which they will be using the language.

Activities

1. In this exercise you are asked to design your own teaching material based on corpus data. Some guidelines on how to approach this task are detailed below:
    *   Identify your audience. Are you teaching beginners, intermediate or advanced students? Are you teaching vocabulary, grammar, lexico-grammar, discourse patterns or literature? What are your students' needs? Are your students learning general English or English for a specific purpose?
    *   Identify a teaching need. Do you want to introduce the use of a new word that you think may be difficult to grasp for your students? Do you want to illustrate the use of an idiom, or a grammatical concept? If students are studying literature, do you want them to look at a specific character in a novel, or compare author style? Decide whether you want to disseminate knowledge that you gained through your study of a corpus, whether you want to design teaching material based on corpus data, and/or whether you want to design an activity for the students to carry out with the help of a corpus.
    *   Choose a corpus that is suitable for your enquiry. Are you looking at speech or writing, literary language or genre specific language. Identify the limitations of your language sample and design your teaching material on the basis of the corpora and resources described in chapter two.
    *   Write a short report describing the rationale behind the design of your material, the design process itself and any problems you encountered on the way.
2. One of the advantages of using corpus analysis with language learners is that it allows students to carry out their own investigations of language in use. This in turn not only empowers the learner but also leads to a degree of interaction with the language that would be difficult to achieve in any other way in the classroom context. Taking the perspective of a language learner, how might the study of the concordance output below taken from the *CANCODE* corpus contribute to the understanding of differences in use between the words *think* and *believe*. Check entries for the two items in any dictionary and assess whether the concordance output gives rise to more, less or different types of meaning. Discuss the value of data-driven learning in relation to: (a) the comparison of the concordance output below with dictionary entries of the same terms; (b) language awareness raising; (c) effectiveness of learning methods; and (d) learner autonomy.

Think:

You'd	**think**	they would.
Because you'd	**think**	you could just walk across the roa
They'll	**think**	Oh, That's organized.
Let's have a	**think**.	
I always	**think**	she looks a bit ill in it.
I always	**think**	it's funny that the Queen has got
is a bit harder but I can	**think**	of some.
I can't	**think**	what to put on this.
I can't	**think**	of anything else.
I didn't	**think**	it would make you drunk you see.
I didn't	**think**	you liked it anyway.
I do	**think**	a lot.
I don't	**think**	it is.
I don't	**think**	so.
I don't	**think**	I do.
Can't even	**think**	of the punchline.
I I I don't honestly	**think**	it'll be a problem.
I	**think**	she was just very drunk.
I	**think**	it might have been on that.
problem on both sides I	**think**.	
like become lovers since I	**think**.	
Just	**think**	when I'm older if I'm not a comple
I never	**think**	of picking or snacking or nibbling
I dread to	**think**.	
It's hard to	**think**	of some of the things about Leeds.
Do you	**think**	they bring the bill?
Do you	**think**	that's it?
What do you	**think**	you're doing?
It's not the first thing you	**think**	of.
Well you	**think**	you're dead funny.
a bit more clout as well you	**think**.	
I don't know what you	**think**	about this procedure
Well it's not what you	**think**	of as a chapel is it.
you get moments when you	**think**	Shit.

Believe:

And like at that age they'd	**believe**	anything and like+
Who'd	**believe**	that.
You'd	**believe**	them.
I'll	**believe**	you.
I can't actually	**believe**	that for the Junior Cert.
But I also	**believe**	that one of the reasons why the
And	**believe**	me when when the police go in an
pier many many years ago and	**believe**	you me if you looked at those
But	**believe**	you me I think it's had a fair
I can	**believe**	it.
Can't	**believe**	you missed that old chestnut.

Can't	**believe**	it.
He can't	**believe**	that its happening to him.
I can't	**believe**	you are watching Carry On films.
I can't	**believe**	that they've said that.
Oh I can't	**believe.**	how many robberies there are.
I still can't	**believe**	it's happened honestly.
I mean I suppose you can't	**believe**	what it was like for you now.
I couldn't	**believe**	that she actually liked them.
I couldn't	**believe**	it.
I couldn't	**believe**	it when I came out and found
She couldn't	**believe**	that I was seventy nine.
I do	**believe**	somebody's knocking on the front
for me because I do	**believe**	there is a lot of money in the
I do I do	**believe**	in it in principle but I've
I don't	**believe**	him.
for me to say cos I don't	**believe**	in killing people and+
I	**believe**	they should.
my previous G P er because I	**believe**	this sort of bias is what closes
But I	**believe**	that now probably the majority
she is trying to make people	**believe**	
But I really	**believe**	they know what it's all about
I was led to	**believe**	It was sealed bids.
You wouldn't	**believe**	it would you.
Can you	**believe**	he's my neighbour?

Further reading

A corpus-based exploration of classroom discourse with a special focus on spoken language can be found in Walsh (2006). There are now a number of studies that highlight the discrepancies between naturally occurring language and traditional language textbooks that are based on invented examples, including Gilmore (2004) and Holmes (1988). In terms of using electronic text resources for teaching and learning, Kettemann and Marko (2002) and Burnard and McEnery (2000) offer a wide ranging collection of articles in this area based on conference proceedings. Willis (2003) offers a practical guide to teaching and learning grammar in the English language classroom which is based on a corpus-based description of the relationship between lexis and grammar.

A discussion of different research genres, partly with reference to the MICASE corpus, and pedagogical applications is covered by Swales (2004).

Discussions of some of the main issues relating to the transferability of corpus-based research and of corpus data into the ELT classroom can be found in Carter (1998), Cook (1998) and Widdowson (1996, 1998).

Research on learner corpora is detailed in Granger (1998) and Granger *et al.* (2002). A number of core issues surrounding the description and collection of English used as a lingua franca are discussed by Seidlhofer (2002).

Notes

1. See Carter (2004) for an overview.
2. See Kettemann for a discussion of *see* and *watch* in the context of vocabulary learning: <http://www-gewi.kfunigraz.ac.at/ed/project/concord2.html>.
3. See chapter two for a description of a selection of learner corpora.
4. This example is based on Adolphs and Durow (2004).

8   Further fields of application

Introduction

The aim of this book has been to provide an overview of some of the methods and resources used in electronic text analysis, and to show how they can be explored to address three particular areas of study: literary texts, ideology and English Language Teaching (ELT). While a comprehensive overview of the many applications that electronic text analysis has in other traditions would be beyond the scope of this publication, the final chapter introduces a number of further key areas in which electronic text analysis is currently being used. These have been selected on the basis of the perceived relevance to the readership of this book. The chapter concludes with a brief discussion of some future challenges for electronic text analysis.

Looking back

When we consider the types of studies reported on in this book, a number of common themes seem to recur. For example, most studies illustrate how electronic text analysis has facilitated textual analysis through the use of software. Widespread access to personal computers and to purpose-built software packages allows a growing circle of user communities to draw on electronic text analysis in their studies. The relative ease with which we can now analyse texts electronically has resulted in a growing interest in the types of methodologies traditionally used by corpus linguists in different disciplines. This expanding circle includes not only those who work in related disciplines where models of language description play a key part, such as ELT for example, but also increasingly researchers in all areas of the arts and humanities and the social sciences.

However, electronic text analysis in such fields is often used to complement other methodologies, sometimes with the aim of cross-triangulation, and sometimes merely as a way of organizing the data or adding some interesting facts to the description of a dataset. The use of different and complementary analytical approaches and methodologies to textual data sets has become common practice in many disciplines.

Corpus linguistics has developed a range of techniques that allow us to extract some types of evidence a lot quicker, such as frequency information for example. It has also developed ways of extracting new kinds of information from electronically stored texts, including semantic prosodies, collocations and multi-word units. The ability to show that a lot of language is phrasal in nature is a pioneering achievement of corpus linguistics.

The aims that may be pursued by people who use electronic text analysis outside of corpus linguistics are likely to be different from those that are concerned purely with language description. As a result the issues that are important to the corpus linguist, such as the careful design and the size of the corpus, may be of less importance in other areas. However, a shift in focus may have an effect on the explanatory power of evidence derived from different data sources that are either too small or unbalanced. The explanatory power of the results generated with the use of corpus linguistic techniques relies on a high level of recurrence. While electronic text analysis used on smaller samples of data or on individual texts may provide us with interesting results, it is important to acknowledge that there may be limitations in terms of the results generated with this type of analysis as far as general language description is concerned.

The value of the use of corpus linguistic techniques outside of corpus linguistics thus has to be judged in relation to the aim of the individual study and the contribution that it makes as part of a framework of diverse methodologies. The use of small-scale corpora for language teaching, as discussed in chapter seven, is a case in point. Tribble (1997) argues that small corpora of around 30,000 words can be useful to increase language awareness of learners and he gives a number of examples of how this may be achieved. The particular value of using corpus techniques in this context is thus related to the successful achievement of the goal, which, in this case, is to raise language awareness.

The individual studies presented in chapters five, six and seven have to be seen in this particular context, that is, in relation to the wider goal of the analysis, and the value they add to other frameworks and approaches that they complement.

Looking sideways

It is inevitable that an introductory book on electronic text analysis can only cover a very limited range of possible areas of application. And since both written and spoken language occupy such key positions in everything we do, the use of electronic text analysis is likely to expand further as new technologies emerge, and as we gain a better understanding of how electronic text analysis may interface with other modes of analysis. Some of the other areas in which electronic text analysis can be a valuable methodology are described below.

The areas of pragmatics and discourse analysis have traditionally focused on short extracts of texts, rather than on extracting patterns from multi-million word corpora. This is partly because the analysis of discourse features is closely tied to the particular place in the ongoing discourse where this feature occurs. An analysis of greetings, for example, would be studied as part of the opening sequence in which they occur. The information about the particular location in a discourse event is, however, lost when we use frequency calculations or concordance outputs to analyse functional features. However, there is now a growing body of research that uses electronic text analysis in pragmatics and discourse analysis and this chapter will illustrate how this methodology might be applied.

Electronic text analysis can also be valuable in the analysis of cultural aspects of language. This is done via a comparison of different language varieties, and will also briefly be discussed. This chapter cannot give a comprehensive overview of these areas but instead aims to illustrate how issues in pragmatics, discourse analysis, and in the study of culture, may be approached through the use of electronic text analysis.

Discourse analysis

The analysis of discourse is a core activity in a range of academic disciplines, including the area of empirically based pragmatics, which will be discussed below. Other disciplines that are concerned with the analysis of discourse are Sociology, Linguistics, Sociolinguistics, Psychology, Philosophy, and some areas of Computer Science. All of these disciplines have developed their own frameworks for the analysis of discourse. Within the linguistics and sociology traditions, discourse analysis is firmly rooted in empirical language data and is concerned with the way in which the social context affects language choices, and how these language choices can be accounted for within different frameworks.

The use of electronic text analysis is a relatively recent methodology used in this area. The benefit of this methodology lies in the way in which it provides discourse analysts with empirical information of specific features that are of interest in the study of discourse. These may include markers of listener feedback, which will be discussed in more detail below, discourse markers, such as *right, now, so*, markers of vague language, and any other items that are related to the organization and negotiation of discourse. An initial comparison of such features in different types of spoken and written texts can be used as evidence for the distributional characteristics of such markers. Following an initial frequency count, an analysis of emerging patterns at the discourse level can help establish the relationship between co-textual and contextual variables and a particular discourse feature that is being analysed. The example of the word *like* below illustrates how frequency information might be used as a way into a more qualitative, functional analysis.[1]

A simple comparison of the 100 most frequent items in a written versus a spoken corpus can give us a good indication of the kinds of lexical items that define these different genres. As discussed in chapter three, a study of the top 100 items in the written component of the *British National Corpus* and in the *CANCODE* spoken corpus immediately shows that a number of items on the spoken list do not appear on the written one. The verb *know*, for example, is the 14th most frequent word in the spoken data but does not occur within the 100 most frequent items in the BNC. Similarly, *yeah* occurs as the 8th most frequent item in the spoken data but is not in the top 100 items in the *BNC*. It is easy enough to guess the reasons for this difference between the two lists. The verb *know* tends to be part of the discourse markers *you know* and *I know*, which can be verified by a concordance search. *Yeah*, on the other hand, is used as a listener feedback token, or 'back-channel' as this feature is often referred to, and is thus unique to spoken discourse. However, even those words that are not obviously linked to either spoken or written discourse at first sight, can be analysed on the basis of different frequencies in the wordlists.

In the frequency list of the *CANCODE* spoken corpus the word *like* occurs as the 28th most frequent word. In contrast, *like* is only the 93rd most frequent word in the 90 million word written component of the *British National Corpus*.[2] This difference in distribution suggests that at least some of the functions of this word are closely tied to spoken discourse. Based on this information, it is now important to study the concordance output to identify those functions that are specific to the spoken discourse context.

Due to the high frequency of this item, the analysis has to be based on a random search of a manageable number of instances. One way of ensuring coverage of the different patterns and meaning senses of a word is to repeat the process of random searches a few times until no new patterns are found in the outputs (see Hunston 2002: 52–3). In the case of *like*, this procedure soon shows that apart from the grammatical roles of *like* as a preposition, conjunction, and as a verb that indicates preferences, *like* also functions as a discourse marker. In the following example it is used to report the speech of other people, as well as that of the speakers themselves:

<S01> Oh right.
<S02> So Jane made me come because she she she'd agreed to go and so she was **like** "I don't want to go there and there are all these hairdressers and me and Benny."
[laughter]
<S02> And that was that. It was really shit and I wish I hadn't agreed to do it. Sat in the chair. After five minutes I was **like** "Yeah. Party" and singing. Making suggestions [laughter]
<S02> Suddenly became the life and soul after sitting there.
<S01> Barmy.

The goal of the conversation here is to entertain the other speakers and to keep the conversation flowing. This is reinforced by the use of reported speech in the anecdote that is being told in this extract. Other elements that add to this goal and to the vividness of the conversation are the use of strong evaluative statements ('It was really shit', 'they are hideous').

Another discourse function of *like* is that of a focusing device in mid sentence, as in the following example:

> <SO1> do you think it is affected by your faith, **like** you were saying you [<S 02> mm] have kind of moral standards of not, **like** hooliganizing and things I mean do you think that's because of of your faith or do you think that's because well because of society or whatever?

The word *like* here is used to provide an example to illustrate a particular point made by the speaker. It is also striking in this example that *like* is used as part of a cluster of vague language, occurring in the vicinity of *and things, I mean* or *whatever*. When we interact with others, there are times where it is necessary to give accurate and precise information; in many informal contexts, however, speakers prefer to convey information which is softened in some way, although such vagueness is often wrongly taken as a sign of careless thinking or sloppy expression. A more accurate term might therefore be *purposefully vague language* (for further discussion, see Eggins and Slade 1997).

Another discourse function of this item is that of requesting further information, as in the extract below:

> <S01> What did I do today. Erm oh. Had a good day today actually. Got loads of stuff sorted out. Finished loads of odds and ends.
> <S02> Did you. **Like** what?
> <S01> **Like** my programme. Finished that off.
> <S02> Which programme?

Like here has a fundamentally analogizing function. It functions to suggest points of comparison or exemplification, even if those comparisons and examples are not actually drawn upon. In such cases, as in the final line in the above extract, *like* also operates to mark a pause before a statement. The analogizing function of *like* is also manifested in phrases such as *like what?* which serves to prompt examples and illustration.

A further function of *like*, which tends to be unique to the use of this word in spoken discourse, is that of a filler, as shown in the following extract:

> <S01> I mean you're all very young but if you just try to think ahead when you're a bit older I mean do you worry about healthcare being made available for you? Do you worry about it?

<S02> Yeah. I think **like** it makes a lot of difference erm cos I mean if you were seriously ill and you went to hospital or something it that service you get it can make so much difference **like** between life and death and you hear about so many things where those extra few minutes or whatever could have made you know all the difference.

This extract shows again the use of *like* surrounded by items of vague language. The topic is relatively serious and *like* is used as a filler that allows the speaker to gain some time to consider what she is about to say.

This analysis has shown how an initial frequency count can be used to identify lexical items that may play a significant role as a discourse marker. A subsequent concordance analysis helps extract those items that appear to have a particular discourse function. As a final step, an analysis of an extended stretch of discourse based on the items identified through the concordance analysis allows us to describe the different discourse functions of the word *like*. Electronic text analysis can thus only facilitate the analysis of discourse to a certain point.

Pragmatics

In the broadest sense, pragmatics is concerned with the relationship between language form, language function and language users. Often, the mere utterances we use to express a particular meaning are indirect, yet our interlocutors are perfectly able to understand what we mean. This is partly so because they can draw on contextual knowledge in their interpretation of our utterances. The classic example of the utterance 'It is cold in here' can be interpreted in various ways depending on the situational context. Thus, if it is said in the context of a meeting where the window is open and there is a chilly draft it may be interpreted as a request to close the window, while in other situations it may be interpreted as a simple observation. Both the level of indirectness used and the interpretation of utterances depends on many variables, including the relationship between the speakers, the situational context and the background knowledge of the speakers.

In terms of pragmatic analysis, a broad distinction can be made between those approaches that use empirical data and those that do not. The former tend to centre around socio-cultural considerations, while the latter are concerned with the analysis of interpretations from a cognitive or philosophical perspective.

The analysis of large datasets of naturally occurring language samples would seem to lend itself to the approach that deals with the relationship between socio-cultural variables (such as gender, status, age, cultural background, etc.) and language form and function. However, because of the various ways in which any one language function can be expressed, it is difficult to pre-determine a set of possible realizations prior to the analysis. Since the starting point of pragmatic investigations tends to be functional in nature, we need some way of identifying lexical items, phrases or syntactical structures that are associated with a particular function (Aijmer 1996). This can be done in various ways, including the use of intuition and elicitation methods. Many speech acts are conventionally indirect, in that they have become associated with a particular indirect formulae. The speech act 'suggestion', for example, is often realized with the use of phrases such as *why don't you, why not, how about*, etc. Once these phrases have been identified, their distribution can be analysed in a corpus.

Another way of identifying forms that are associated with a particular function is to analyse an extended stretch of discourse and develop a tagging system for individual speech acts. This procedure has been briefly discussed in chapter five in relation to literary discourse. Similar projects are currently underway that have developed functional tagging systems for non-literary discourse.[3] Future work in this area may be able to suggest a more automated way for the identification of the illocutionary force of some utterances, which refers to the effect that a speaker's utterance has upon the world. For example, in the case of the utterance mentioned above, 'It is cold in here', the illocutionary force might be that of a request. At present, such an effect cannot be identified automatically but requires a close analysis of the on-going discourse and discourse context, as well as the study of conventionalized expressions that are routinely linked to a particular illocutionary force.

There are, of course, some speech acts that are associated with smaller sets of linguistic realizations than others, such as expressions of gratitude for example. These can be studied with the use of a corpus more readily (Schauer and Adolphs 2006). But even with speech acts that are associated with a somewhat larger linguistic repertoire, such as suggestions for example, electronic text analysis can contribute interesting insights to the analysis.

As already mentioned there are a number of different phrases associated with making suggestions, with varying degrees of directness. However, rather than assigning levels of directness on an intuitive basis, the analysis of corpus data allows us to shift the focus to what is appropriate usage in particular contexts. Figure 8.1 shows the frequency of occurrence of these phrases in a 500,000-word corpus of conversations in the intimate category of the CANCODE corpus that contains interactions between speakers who know one another very well (e.g. members of a family, partners, etc). Subsequent analysis of the individual instances also shows the different types of functions realized by the individual phrases. The dark colour in the bars indicates the frequency with which the individual sequences function as questions while the light colour shows the function of suggestion.

While the overall numbers of the individual forms are somewhat low, an interesting picture emerges about the distribution of the forms. In particular, the marked difference between *suggest* and *why don't you* shows that *why don't you* might be the preferred form in situations where the participants are in close relationships

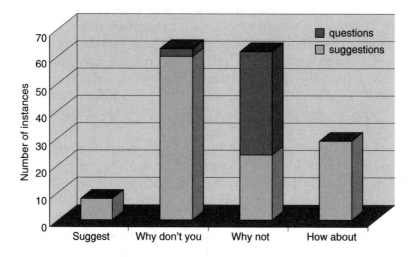

Figure 8.1 Frequency of speech act phrases and their function in the context category *close friends and family*.

with respect to this particular corpus. Another interesting outcome of the analysis above is the extent to which particular phrases are associated with a specific function. We can see, for example, that *why not* is routinely used in the corpus to introduce genuine questions, as well as to make suggestions, while *how about* and *why don't you* are more strongly associated with the function of making suggestions. This type of analysis gives rise to a description of such phrases that is based on different assumptions to those that underlie traditional pragmatic descriptions. According to the latter, *why don't you* would be analysed as a direct speech act if it was used to introduce a question and thus congruent with its syntactic form. However, it would be seen as an indirect speech act if it functioned as a suggestion, as here the syntactic form would not be congruent with the form of a suggestion. A corpus-based analysis, on the other hand, would not analyse the level of indirectness in terms of syntactic structure, but rather in terms of distribution in a particular discourse context. The individual phrases would be analysed in relation to their core functions and their grammatical integration would be used as a further pointer as to the type of speech act they are likely to realize (see also DeClerck 2004 for a corpus-based analysis of the different functions of *let's*). It should be noted that while these phrases may be related to the speech act *suggestion*, they are not functional synonymous. Instead, as we have seen in this example, their use tends to be associated with different situations and with a difference in force.

The use of electronic text analysis to support pragmatic investigations of the relationship between speakers, context and level of directness/indirectness of an utterance is still relatively under-explored. This is mainly because of the difficulty in linking language form to utterance force. However, functional analyses of individual lexical items or phrases can provide an empirical angle on some of the core issues in pragmatics, including the difference between direct and indirect speech acts.

Electronic text analysis and culture

Culture and language are inextricably intertwined and the study of empirical language data should be able to provide some evidence of this relationship. Traces of culture in language can be both of lexico-grammatical and pragmatic nature. As such, we may find differing levels of indirectness in the realization of individual speech acts in different cultures for example. In terms of individual lexical items and phrases that convey traces of cultural attitudes and beliefs, Carter (1998: 49), for example, highlights the types of phrases used in British English that make reference to other European nations in this context, such as *Dutch courage* and *French leave*. While these types of idioms are unlikely to yield high frequencies in a corpus, there are a number of areas of language use that are likely to produce more frequent occurrences. One of these is in the area of active listenership, which will be discussed in more detail in the next section as an example of cultural reflexes in language.

Conversations typically contain listener responses, such as short utterances and non-verbal surrogates. These 'accompaniment signals', according to Kendon (1967), are produced by the listener as an accompaniment to a speaker when s/he is talking at length, and there is evidence that the speaker relies upon these for guidance as to how the message is being received. Observations of both verbal and non-verbal behaviour while listening (e.g. Goodwin 1981) tell us that listeners respond with precision at appropriate moments and in appropriate ways to incoming talk. Yngve (1970) introduced the term 'back channel' to refer to the 'short messages' that a speaker receives while holding the floor. He too points to the importance of these messages as markers of quality in ongoing communication. A general distinction can be made between vocalizations, such as *mhm* and *uhu*, and lexicalized back-channels, such as *absolutely*, *excellent*, *yes*, etc.

In the following conversation between three cleaners in a University hall of residence talk about cleaning student bedrooms. Speaker <S03> complains about the students' behaviour towards the cleaners while speakers <S02> and <S01> signal involved listenership throughout this discourse episode:

<S03> Well the fridge probably was+
<S02> [unintelligible]
<S03> +cos I mean I I didn't clean the fridge.
<S02> Yeah. But it can be bad an hour after.
<S03> But I er I cleaned all the all the thing and mopped all the floors+
<S02> **Mm.**

<S03> +in the morning. I mean what annoys me it puts you off doing any-
thing.

<S01> **Mhm.**

<S03> What annoys me is that if a student comes up to me and says Can you
clean tomorrow or Can you clean an hour, half an hour later. And you
turn round and you say Yes.

<S01> Mhm.

<S03> And then the problem with it is you're willing to do something for
them.

<S01> **Yeah.**

<S02> And then what do they do for you?

<S01> Nothing.

<S03> **No.**

The discourse flow that emerges from this type of listenership shows a high degree
of convergence, to the extent that it becomes difficult to distinguish between back-
channel items which signal attention and those that signal agreement or some kind
of emotive response.

One of the problems with using text-based corpora in the analysis of
backchannels is the lack of prosodic information that can make it difficult to
classify different types of vocalization. However, there are also a number of
lexicalized backchannels that include both single word items and multi-word
clusters.

In the following extract two female teachers in their forties discuss the way in
which one of their fellow teachers deals with a difficult class of pupils:

<S02> There's one or two as I say nasty elements you know in there. And they
seem and But Seven E H I know Annie teaches them and er cos she
had them in a while for P S E. And sh= you know she was tearing her
hair out with them.

<S01> **Really.**

<S02> Mm. I mean she's an ex deputy head yet she'd had+

<S01> Erm I think

<S02> +enough as well by the end of term. [laughs] And I thought God if

<S01> I think that gets Maggie down as well cos she [unintelligible]. [laughs]

<S02> **That's right.**

<S01> She's very keen.

<S02> **Absolutely.**

<S01> And she gets fed up when they're being+

<S02> **I would.**

<S01> +told off all day.

<S02> I would. After this term with sort of total mixed ability for French I would just have a sink class quite honestly. And apparently this Mrs Thompson who's coming she she wants to stream for French or set them for French.

The extract above shows a more involved style of active listenership that includes individual lexicalized items such as *really* and *absolutely*, as well as multi-word sequences such as *that's right*.

In terms of language and culture, O'Keeffe and Adolphs (forthcoming) highlight a number of different forms of backchannels which can be found in a corpus of spoken Irish English but which are not present in a corpus of spoken British English. One example is the multi-word sequence *are you serious*. The following example from O'Keeffe and Adolphs (forthcoming) shows how this sequence is used as a backchannel in Irish English. In this extract three speakers are talking about two young men in their community who have built a house together:

<S01> ... but uh we went out in last night and we went back to Morgan's house. Morgan is Trevor's best friend since they were knee high and the two of them+

<S02> And are the two of them?

<S03> Morgan Morgan who cabinet makers do we know him?

<S01> Am Morgan.

<S02> Murphy.

<S03> It's not Morgan Murphy. is it Morgan Murphy? I'd know him all right.

<S01> I don't know. People keep on saying that.

<S03> Is he a tall chap? Tall chap dark hair? dark hair and he's also pretty pretty broad yeah yeah I'd say it's Morgan Murphy by the sound of it.

<S01> He's twenty. He'd be twenty-nine as well a year older than Niamh and he's from down there.

<S02> Yeah his mum used to be a national school teacher.
... [nine turns later after a digression about Morgan's relations] ...

<S01> Well anyway he's got he's just built his house it was built in the last six months my god it's a massive yoke the two lads living on their own.

<S02> *Are you serious?*

<S01> Yes you would be afraid to touch anything.

<S02> Aren't they marvellous.

<S01> Yeah really like it doesn't look like a home at all cause everything is just perfect.

<S03> Like a showhouse.

O'Keeffe and Adolphs (forthcoming) note that the fact that this particular form of back-channel does not occur in the British English corpus, might lead to cross-cultural pragmatic failure (see Thomas 1983) as it might be misinterpreted by a speaker of British English as an evaluation of the propositional content of the previous speaker's utterance.

There are other forms of backchannels that show a direct correlation with a particular variety of English. Figure 8.2 shows the frequencies of non-minimal response tokens in a component of the Limerick Corpus of Irish English (LCIE) comprising 20,000 words of casual conversation between young female speakers.[4,5]

As we can see from this table, there is a preponderance of religious references in the data, including *(Oh/my) God, Jesus (Christ)* and *God help us*. These are examples of cultural reflexes in one of the most common functions of casual spoken interaction, i.e. that of indicating active listenership. In a recent study of non-minimal responses in British and American spoken English, these religious references are notably absent (McCarthy 2003). This observation provides further evidence for the close relationship between these particular forms of active listenership and the culture in which they are used.

While the brief discussion above has focused on relatively obvious forms in terms of cultural values, there are a number of studies that illustrate how the analysis of less marked lexical items reveal cultural differences between two languages. Tognini-Bonelli and Manca (2004) investigate the translation equivalence of individual lexical items based on English and Italian information websites on farmhouse holidays for holiday makers. Using a concordance analysis of words such as *welcome* for example, the authors are able to show differences in the co-selection with other items. In the British holiday corpus, the use of *welcome* in relation to the word *children* often occurs in a context where particular restrictions are made, for example with reference to the age of the children that are welcomed. In the Italian corpus, on the other hand, there is no direct translation equivalence of the use of *welcome* in relation to *children*. The authors argue that this might suggest that the

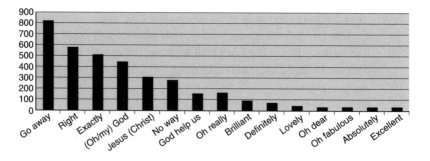

Figure 8.2 Frequencies of non-minimal response tokens in a 20,000 word sample of the Limerick corpus of Irish English.

presence of children is taken for granted in the Italian context while there are notable restrictions and limitations imposed when it comes to the use of the word *children* in the British context, which in turn can be interpreted with reference to cultural differences.

The examples above highlight the potential contribution that electronic text analysis has to offer to the study of culture. With an increasing number of spoken and written corpora that mirror different varieties of a particular language, such as the *ICE* corpora for example, there are now ample resources available to support this kind of investigation. The same applies to parallel corpora, where the analysis of translation equivalence can be explored in relation to linguistic traces of culture.

Looking ahead

With advances in technology, the use of electronic text analysis in the humanities and in the social sciences is likely to become increasingly prominent. The methodologies developed in the area of corpus linguistics might offer a helpful approach to many research questions that are not solely concerned with advancing language description in one way or another. However, it may prove that the use of such methodologies is best combined with other types of approaches, such as the ones described in this chapter under the heading discourse analysis for example. The role that other approaches play, including that of intuition, and how different approaches relate to one another, will be a matter for future exploration in this area.

One of the key issues in this context will be our definition of text. What is the impact of using hypertext as part of our investigations? Do we need to change the goal posts of electronic text analysis and of corpus compilation to include 'texts within texts' that are represented through links on a webpage for example? What about the use of images which form part of a text in certain documents. Can electronic text analysis only be applied to pure textual documents or is there a way of taking into account visual elements of a text? The pioneering developments of the 'web as corpus' projects may be able to start shedding some light on these issues.

Similarly, with the analysis of spoken discourse, is a purely textual analysis ever going to be sufficient to derive significant patterns of communication? If we consider the example of listener feedback above, it soon becomes clear that an investigation based on the text stream alone restricts our analysis to a degree that may make the results questionable. While we have only compared lexicalized response tokens, a comprehensive analysis of listener feedback has to include vocalizations that are best represented with the use of prosodic information. But even with lexicalized response tokens, intonation and gesture are key elements that contribute to the overall function of the item, i.e. whether a listener response is interpreted as an acknowledgement of information or as an engaged response token signalling surprise or some other, more involved feedback item.

The three areas in which many of the future challenges in electronic text analysis lie are thus:

- **Data collection**. What are the key sites at which we collect electronic texts? Will the internet become a main resource for corpus linguistics? What are the copyright and ethical considerations that we need to consider in the development of electronic text collections? What types of data do we collect? How do we deal with hypertext in electronic text analysis? Do we need to collect other types of data to complete our datasets, such as video data and audio data in the case of verbal interaction? How do electronic texts interface with other qualitative and quantitative datasets in the arts and humanities? And can they be analysed in a complementary way? How much data is required for different types of electronic text analysis and for different research purposes? How does the size of the electronic text resource affect analytical results?
- **Data representation**. How do we represent textual data for different analytical purposes and for different disciplines? How do we represent different data streams, including textual, visual and audio streams? What are the implications of different types of representation for our analysis and for the results of our analysis? What are the implications of using tagged and parsed corpora, and how do we best link meta-data to our text collections?
- **Data replay and analysis**. What kinds of interfaces for electronic text analysis best facilitate data analysis in different disciplines and for different groups of users? How can data resources and analyses be shared by different users, and what are the ethical implications of this process. How do different types of analysis relate to electronic text analysis?

These are just a few of the key questions that will have to be addressed in some detail as the interest in the use of electronic text analysis grows in different disciplines. The types of methodologies that have been developed in the area of corpus linguistics will play a major part in these discussions, as their relevance to different areas within applied linguistics and in other disciplines is being further explored. This book has tried to provide a basic introduction to some of these techniques with the aim of both illustrating their application and highlighting some of the issues that arise from such applications.

Summary

One of the recurrent themes throughout the book has been the relationship between different types of electronic text data, methodologies and research purposes. One of the main aims pursued in the area of corpus linguistics is the identification of language patterns with a view to establish better language descriptions.

This, however, is not necessarily the main aim in other disciplines and in other areas of applied linguistics. The value of particular methodologies and types of electronic text collections therefore has to be assessed in relation to the overall research aim and other methods that might be applied as part of the overall investigation.

Three further areas in which electronic text analysis can be a useful approach have been discussed in this chapter: discourse analysis, pragmatics and the analysis of language and culture. The sample studies in this chapter have shown how electronic text analysis might be applied in these areas and how it might interface with other, more traditional methodologies. In disciplines that deal predominantly with the qualitative analysis of spoken discourse, electronic text analysis may be used as an additional source of evidence, which can provide a way in to more qualitative types of analyses.

The chapter has further listed a range of challenges that have to be addressed in order to achieve a more seamless integration of corpus methods in other areas of applied linguistics, humanities and social sciences. These centre around issues of data collection, data representation and data replay and analysis, all of which are central to the discussions in the different chapters of this book. The scope of electronic text analysis as outlined in this publication then has to be assessed in relation to the datasets, annotation systems and computer software and hardware currently available. With rapid advances and developments in all of these areas the scope of electronic text analysis is likely to expand considerably over the next decade, and the focus might shift towards fields of application that are just starting to draw on this type of methodology to answer the questions relevant to their own disciplines. At the same time the methodology that is referred to as electronic text analysis in this book is likely to be adapted to include systematic exploitation of other data-streams, such as video and audio data along with textual renderings. This book has aimed to provide a general introduction to the way in which texts can be analysed electronically in order to provide additional evidence to support language description and exploration in different areas. At the same time it has offered a general background against which some of the basic questions related to data collection, representation and analysis might be considered.

Activities

1. Carry out a study of all the phrases you can think of that can be used to signal agreement with, or positive assessment of a proposition. You may wish to draw on the *Michigan Corpus of Academic Spoken English* (MICASE) for this purpose.[6] What are the frequency distributions of different phrases in different (academic) contexts? Discuss possible reasons for the different distributions. Now study the concordance data for individual phrases and note down any common

patterns. Is there anything in the immediate co-text of the phrases that reinforces their occurrence in particular (academic) contexts?

2.   Take one particular form of a lexicalized listener response item, such as *right*
     or *yeah* for example, and make a list of all the factors that might affect the way
     in which this particular response is interpreted by the main speaker. Now
     carry out a concordance search of the particular item in any of the online
     spoken corpora discussed in this book. Alternatively, study the random
     sample of the listener response item *yeah* in the output from the *CANCODE*
     corpus below:

+every day. Yeah. <S01>	**Yeah.**	Oh right. <S02> So guess it
And we're there. <S01>	**Yeah**	right. <S02> Erm Mark was
Rather than being+ <S01>	**Yeah.**	<S02> [Unintelligible] <S01> Yeah.
<S02> I'm afraid not. <S01>	**Yeah.**	It's just that er my daughter's
<S02> proper writing. <S01>	**Yeah.**	That's everything
<S02> Oh yeah. <S01>	**Yeah.**	That's great.
<S02> One first class. <S01>	**Yeah.**	And then this one er to Sweden
<S02> Sesame prawn toast. <S01>	**Yeah.**	<S03> Can we have a selection
<S02> Oh are you? <S01>	**Yeah.**	<S02> What you watching?
<S02> Thank you. <S01>	**Yeah.**	<S02> There you go.
<S02> I were wondering+ <S01>	**Yeah.**	<S02> +if you could do me a favour
<S03> Simon? <S02> Yeah. <S01>	**Yeah.**	I'll bring some fresh glasses as

On the basis of this small sample, assess the validity of a purely textual approach
to the analysis of active listernership that is solely based on concordance data. What
are the advantages and what are the limitations of such an approach and is there
any way in which the they can be reconciled?

Further reading

For an overview of some of the key issues and challenges that corpus linguistics in
particular and electronic text analysis in general will continue to be concerned
with, see chapter McEnery and Wilson (2001, chapter 7) and Sinclair (2004a,
chapter twelve). The use of corpus linguistics in the area of discourse analysis is
discussed in detail in Conrad (2002). For an accessible account of many of the areas
of application discussed in this chapter in the domain of media discourse see
O'Keeffe (forthcoming).

Notes

1.   This example is based on Adolphs and Carter (2003).
2.   The frequency count for *like* in the *BNC* has been taken from the companion website
     to Leech *et al.* (2001) at <http://www.comp.lancs.ac.uk/ucrel/ bncfreq/>.

3. See for example the UCREL project on automatic speech act tagging described at <http://www.comp.lancs.ac.uk/computing/research/ucrel/projects.html#spaac>.

4. For a description of this resource see Farr *et al.* (2004).

5. I am grateful to Anne O'Keeffe for allowing me to use this research which will be published in full in O'Keeffe (forthcoming).

6. The searchable web-interface for the MICASE corpus can be accessed at <http://micase.umdl.umich.edu/cgi/m/micase/micase-idx?type=revise>. A sample analysis of suggestions as a functional category based on the MICASE corpus has been carried out by John Swales and can be accessed at <http://www.lsa.umich.edu/eli/micase/How_to_function.htm>.

Appendix 1   Transcription conventions and codes in the CANCODE data

Transcription conventions of spoken interactions vary depending on the research purpose of the respective project for which they are used. As highlighted in chapter two, a useful representation of spoken discourse is highly dependent on careful transcription and, even then, it has to be acknowledged that textual renderings of spoken interaction can never provide a completely accurate picture of the event. This is due to a number of reasons, some of which relate to the multi-modal nature of spoken discourse which is not yet integrated into spoken corpora, and others relate to the fact that there is always a level of interpretation involved in any type of transcription.

Since a substantial number of examples of spoken discourse throughout the book are taken from the CANCODE corpus, this appendix serves as a guide to the transcription conventions and codes used for this corpus. For information on individual codes used in examples and concordance lines taken from other corpora in this book, please refer to the respective web-sites of these corpora.

The transcriptions of the CANCODE corpus do not include prosodic information. For the purpose of this book some of the original transcription conventions have been kept in the extracts and concordance lines that have been used, while others have been changed or deleted to aid ease of reading of selected extracts.

Transcription convention	Symbol	Explanation
Speaker codes	<S01>, <S02>	Each speaker is numbered with separate codes.
Extralinguistic information	[ ]	This includes laughter, coughs and transcribers' comments about speech on the tape, including notes on anonymized elements, e.g. [company name]
Interrupted sentence	+	When an utterance is interrupted by another speaker this is indicated by using a + sign at the end of the interrupted utterance and at the point where the speaker resumes his or her utterance:

<S01> You could +
<S02> Yeah
<S01> + come round tonight

Unfinished words	=	Where speakers change their course in the middle of individual words, this has been marked as follows:

<S01> And there was a s= a slight risk then...

Punctuation	. ? ,	A full stop or question mark is used to mark the end of a sentence (depending on intonation). 'Sentences' are anything that is felt to be a complete utterance, such as:

<S02> Erm is MX there?
<S01> He's got somebody with him at the moment MX.
<S02> Right.

'Right' is considered as a sentence here. A comma indicates that the speaker has re-cast what he/she was saying, including false starts, e.g.:

<S01> That's not, that can't be true.

Glossary

Annotation   Analytical information that is added to electronic and machine readable texts. This extra information is added in the form of codes in the same manner as in MARK-UP. TAGGING and PARSING are both forms of annotation.

Chi-square test   Like a LOG-LIKELIHOOD analysis, this is a measure of statistical significance which can be used to derive the KEYWORDs for a particular TARGET CORPUS. The calculation involves the comparison of an item from a target corpus with its equivalent in a REFERENCE CORPUS and thus comparing its observed frequency against its expected frequency. If the difference between observed and expected frequencies is large, then the occurrence of the item in the target corpus can be thought to be significant.

Colligation   The patterns of co-occurrence of words with particular grammatical items.

Collocation   The tendency of particular words to co-occur within a language more frequently than would be expected by chance. Certain words can therefore be seen to be lexically attracted to one another; for example 'rancid' collocates with 'butter'.

Competence   In Chomskyan linguistics, this refers to a speaker-listener's internalized and intuitive knowledge of a language as opposed to their PERFORMANCE of it.

Concordance   A concordance lists the occurrences of a particular search item in a corpus in the context of the surrounding text that occurs alongside the item. This can be used to observe COLLOCATION patterns, COLLIGATION patterns and SEMANTIC PROSODY. See also KWIC, NODE and SPAN.

Corpus (plural **Corpora**)   A collection of linguistic data, such as written texts or transcribed speech, that has been designed to be representative of a particular language domain or variety, with its size and content having been carefully taken into account. This careful design and consideration of representativeness differentiates corpora from other electronic text resources, such as

TEXT ARCHIVES. Most contemporary corpora exist in a machine readable form so that patterns of occurrence of lexical and grammatical items can be derived through computer-aided analysis.

Corpus-based   In this approach to corpus analysis, the researcher uses the data provided by the corpus to test a previously established hypothesis – as opposed to a CORPUS DRIVEN approach (see Tognini-Bonelli 2001).

Corpus-driven   In this approach to corpus analysis, it is the data and patterns generated by the corpus that dictate what is studied by the researcher – as opposed to a CORPUS BASED approach (see Tognini–Bonelli 2001).

Corpus linguistics   Investigates language based on large sets of naturally occurring language data (see CORPUS) with the aim of gaining a better understanding of language in use (see PERFORMANCE).

Electronic Text Analysis   Used here as an umbrella term for any type of analysis that draws on digitized texts including the process of adding analytical and contextual information to such texts. This term is not linked to a specific tradition such as CORPUS LINGUISTICS or HUMANITIES COMPUTING.

Empiricism   Where investigation into a particular area or subject is based on the observation of data as it occurs in the real world and which is therefore external to the researcher's intuition – as opposed to RATIONALISM.

General Corpus   This is a CORPUS that includes many different types of texts with an aim of giving a large-scale, general representation of a language – as opposed to a SPECIALIZED CORPUS. These corpora are often assembled with an aim to produce reference materials such as dictionaries and can thus often be used as a REFERENCE CORPUS.

Historical Corpus   This is a CORPUS that includes texts from different periods of time and which can thus enable the researcher to analyse historical changes in the language.

Humanities computing   This is an approach that investigates how technology can be used for research into humanities subjects. It is particularly concerned with enhancing and documenting textual interpretations through computer-based analysis and annotation, often within a hermeneutic tradition.

Idiom principle   This operates when speakers make use of lexicalized and semi-lexicalized phrases that are stored whole in the long term memory and retrieved as single items – as opposed to the OPEN CHOICE PRINCIPLE.

Keywords   (a) The search word investigated in a concordance study; (b) Keywords refer to those items that occur with a significantly higher frequency (positive keywords) or with a significantly lower frequency (negative keywords) in a text or collection of texts when compared with a larger REFERENCE CORPUS (see Scott 1997, 2003). This helps to explain what characterizes particular discourses, such as the high frequency of words like 'antibiotics' in health professional discourse as compared to everyday conversation (see chapter three). They can be derived statistically from corpora through a LOG-LIKLIHOOD analysis or a CHI-SQUARE TEST; (c) The term 'key word' is sometimes used in a different sense where it refers to lexical items or phrases that have been identified by the analyst to have a particular relevance to a research topic, such as the word *gay* in a study of the representation of homosexual men.

KWIC   (Key Word in Context) A standard way of presenting concordance data for a particular lexical item or phrase, where the search word or keyword appears in the middle of the line with its co-text on either side. See also CON-CORDANCE, NODE and SPAN.

Learner corpus   A CORPUS that includes texts, either spoken or written, produced by learners of a particular language.

Lemma   The headword for all the possible inflections of that word. For example, the lemma SAY includes the word-forms *say, saying, said, says*. Different forms of the same lemma tend to vary significantly in terms of their overall frequency, with one particular form tending to be more frequent than others. See also WORD FAMILIES.

Log-likelihood   Like a CHI-SQUARE TEST, this is a measure of statistical significance which can be used to identify KEYWORDs in a text or collection of texts. The calculation involves comparing an item from a TARGET COR-PUS with its equivalent in the REFERENCE CORPUS and thus comparing the observed frequency of the item against its expected frequency.

Mark-up   The process of adding consistent codes to a text which give information about its typography and layout. Mark-up information is generally represented through angle brackets, such as <p_> to indicate a new paragraph. In a spoken corpus, mark-up codes can be used to indicate individual speakers and interruptions for example.

Meta-data   Structured data that is used to describe other data, such as that stored in a corpus of texts.

Monitor corpus   A CORPUS to which new texts are added at regular intervals. This constantly growing text database can be used to observe changes in the language.

Multivariate analysis   The statistical analysis of data which involves investigating the relationship between multiple variables.

Multi-word units   Sequences of interrelated words that occur together more frequently than they would by chance and which are retrieved as single lexical units (see also IDIOM-PRINCIPLE). They occur with varying degrees of fixedness and incorporate a range of forms such as formulae (e.g. *have a nice day*), metaphors (e.g. *kick the bucket*) and COLLOCATIONs (e.g. *rancid butter*).

Mutual information   A statistical method that can be used to derive COLLOCATIONs of particular words and the degree of their lexical attraction. The calculation involves comparing the expected probability of co-occurrence of two items in a corpus with their actual, observed frequency of co-occurrence. The ratio between expected and observed frequency is termed Mutual Information.

Natural Language Processing (NLP)   Studies how computers can be made to process and interpret naturally occurring text. This approach tends to be concerned with the design of particular applications, such as spell checkers or machine translation software for example.

Node   The search item in a concordance study which appears in the centre of the page in a concordance output with the words that co-occur with it appearing on either side (the SPAN). See also KWIC.

Open-choice principle   Where linguistic choices are made based on grammatical rules and words are selected to fill a particular 'slot' – as opposed to the IDIOM PRINCIPLE.

Parallel corpus   A CORPUS that includes texts in at least two different languages that have either been directly translated or that have been produced in the different languages for the same purpose.

Parsing   A form of ANNOTATION where the text is annotated for its functional categories on the basis of the Part of Speech information assigned in TAGGING.

Part of speech   This is the category that a word is assigned to based on the grammatical function that it performs within a clause, such as a noun, a verb, an adjective, an adverb, a pronoun, a preposition or a conjunction. Electronic text resources can be TAGGED to indicate which part of speech each word belongs to.

Performance   This denotes a speaker's actual use of a language in a real-life context. It is the opposite of language COMPETENCE.

Qualitative analysis   Making observations about data in terms of qualities or characteristics. It is descriptive rather than numerical. As opposed to QUANTITATIVE ANALYSIS.

Quantitative analysis   Making observations about data in terms of numbers, quantities or measurements. As opposed to QUALITATIVE ANALYSIS.

Rationalism   Where investigation into and judgements about a particular subject are based on the researcher's intuition and reasoning – as opposed to EMPIRICISM.

Reference corpus   A large CORPUS, often used to determine the language patterns that are general across a language, against which a smaller, TARGET CORPUS can be compared.

Semantic prosody   This concept describes the associations that arise from the collocates of a particular lexical item – if it tends to occur with a negative co-text then the item will have negative shading and if it tends to occur with a positive co-text then it will have positive shading.

Span   The words or items that surround the central search item, the NODE, in CONCORDANCE data. The span is often set to include four to five words to either side of the NODE.

Specialised corpus   This is a CORPUS that includes texts that belong to a particular type, such as academic discourse like the *Michigan Corpus of Academic spoken English*, the discourse of a particular age group like *COLT* (*The Bergen Corpus of London Teenage Language*) or the discourse of a particular profession such as the talk between health-care professionals and patients – as opposed to a GENERAL CORPUS.

T-score   A statistical method that can be used to measure the significance of difference between observed and expected frequencies of items in corpus data.

Tagging   A form of ANNOTATION where each word in a text or CORPUS is annotated with a code in order to provide linguistic information about which PART OF SPEECH the word represents.

Target corpus   The CORPUS whose particular discourse characteristics are being investigated and often compared against a larger, REFERENCE CORPUS.

Text archive   Like a CORPUS, this is a large collection of texts which may exist in an electronic, machine-readable format but which, unlike corpora, has not been specifically designed for linguistic study.

Tokens   This refers to the number of running words in a text – every word that occurs is therefore included in the count. See also TYPES.

Types   This refers to the number of different words in a text – only the number of unique word forms will therefore be counted, not their repetitions. See also TOKENS.

Word families   Include all the derivations and inflections of a particular lexical stem. For example, the words happy, happiness and unhappy would all be included in the same word family. See also LEMMA.

Z-score   A statistical method that can be used to measure the significance of difference between observed and expected frequencies of items in corpus data.

Bibliography of websites

Please note that the URLs below were accurate at the time of writing. For updated information please refer to the companion website to the book.

Companion Website to the Book

http://www.routledge.com/textbooks/0415320216

Websites referred to in text

Australian Corpus of English
Description and manual for the corpus:
http://khnt.hit.uib.no/icame/manuals/ace/
Available on ICAME CD-ROM: http://nora.hd.uib.no/ corpora.html

BASE (British Academic Spoken English Corpus)
Website: http://www.rdg.ac.uk/AcaDepts/ll/base_corpus/

BNC (British National Corpus)
Website: http://www.natcorp.ox.ac.uk/
Online search facility (limited to 50 random instances):
http://sara.natcorp.ox.ac.uk/lookup.html
Frequency lists of the British National Corpus can be accessed via the companion website to Leech *et al.* (2001) at http://www.comp.lancs.ac.uk/ ucrel/bncfreq/

Brown Corpus
Description:
http://clwww.essex.ac.uk/w3c/corpus_ling/content/corpora/list/private/brown/brown.html

Cambridge International Corpus
Website: http://www.cambridge.org/elt/corpus/international_corpus.htm

Cambridge Learner Corpus
Website (description of corpus):
http://www.cambridge.org/elt/corpus/learner_corpus.htm

CANCODE (Cambridge and Nottingham Corpus of Discourse in English)
Website: http://www.cambridge.org/elt/corpus/cancode.htm

COBUILD (Collins and Birmingham University International Language Database) – also referred to as the Bank of English
Description of the COBUILD project: http://www.collins.co.uk/books.aspx?group=140

Collins WordbanksOnline
Website: http://www.collins.co.uk/corpus/corpussearch.aspx

COLT (Bergen Corpus of London Teenage Language) – (constituent of the BNC)
Website: http://torvald.aksis.uib.no/colt/

DIPEx (Database of Individual Patient Experiences)
Website: http://www.dipex.org/

FLOB (Freiburg-LOB Corpus of British English)
Description and manual for the corpus: http://khnt.hit.uib.no/icame/manuals/flob/INDEX.HTM

FROWN (Freiburg-Brown Corpus of American English)
Description and manual for the corpus: http://khnt.hit.uib.no/icame/manuals/frown/index.htm
Codes for the corpus:
http://khnt.hit.uib.no/icame/manuals/frown/CODE.HTM
Available on ICAME CD-ROM: http://nora.hd.uib.no/ corpora.html

The Helsinki Corpus
Manual can be accessed at:
http://khnt.hit.uib.no/icame/manuals/HC/INDEX.HTM

ICE (International Corpus of English)
Website: http://www.ucl.ac.uk/english-usage/ice/index.htm
A sample of the British component of the corpus can be downloaded at:
http://www.ucl.ac.uk/english-usage/ice-gb/sampler/

ICLE (International Corpus of Learners' English)
http://www.fltr.ucl.ac.be/fltr/germ/etan/cecl/Cecl-Projects/Icle/icle.htm

Kolhapur Corpus
> Description and manual the corpus: http://khnt.hit.uib.no/icame/manuals/kolhapur/ INDEX.HTM
> Available on ICAME CD-ROM at: http://nora.hd.uib.no/corpora.html

Limerick Corpus of Irish English (LCIE)
> http://www.ul.ie/~lcie/homepage.htm

LOB (Lancaster-Oslo/Bergen Corpus)
> Description:
>> http://clwww.essex.ac.uk/w3c/corpus_ling/content/corpora/list/private/LOB/ lob.html

London-Lund Corpus
> Description:
>> http://khnt.hit.uib.no/icame/manuals/LONDLUND/INDEX.HTM
> Available on ICAME CD-ROM at: http://nora.hd.uib.no/corpora.html

Longman Corpus Network (group of databases)
> http://www.longman.com/dictionaries/corpus/lccont.html

Longman Learners' Corpus of written English
> Description of corpus:
>> http://www.longman.com/dictionaries/corpus/lclearn.html

MICASE (Michigan Corpus of Academic Spoken English)
> http://www.lsa.umich.edu/eli/micase/index.htm
> Browse the corpus: http://www.hti.umich.edu/m/micase/browse.html
> Concordance Search Engine:
>> http://www.hti.umich.edu/cgi/m/micase/micase-idx?type=revise

OTA (Oxford Text Archive) – Access to archive online
> http://ota.ahds.ac.uk/

Project Gutenberg – Online searchable database of e-texts
> http://www.promo.net/pg/

SCOTS (Scottish Corpus of Texts and Speech) – Access to corpus online.
> http://www.scottishcorpus.ac.uk/
> Online search facility: http://www.scottishcorpus.ac.uk/corpus/search/

The Switchboard Corpus
> http://www.cavs.msstate.edu/hse/ies/projects/switchboard/

Survey of English Usage
>   http://www.ucl.ac.uk/english-usage/

TAPoR (Text-Analysis Portal for Research)
>   http://tapor.ca
>   Demo of word frequencies and concordances: http://test-tapor.mcmaster.ca/
>   TaporMain/portal/portal

VOICE (Vienna-Oxford International Corpus of English)
>   http://www.univie.ac.at/Anglistik/voice/
>   Examples of transcriptions and mark-up conventions: http://www.univie.ac.at/
>   Anglistik/voice/

Wellington Corpus
>   Description and manual for the corpus: http://khnt.hit.uib.no/icame/manuals/
>   wellman/INDEX.HTM
>   Available on ICAME CD-ROM at: http://nora.hd.uib.no/corpora.html

The web as corpus

WebCorp Project
>   Allows users to specify a search word, phrase or pattern and to further specify
>   the domain of discourse on which the search will be based –
>   http://www.webcorp.org.uk/

Annotation and mark-up

CLAWS (Constituent Likelihood Automatic Word-tagging System)
>   http://www.comp.lancs.ac.uk/computing/research/ucrel/claws/

Codes for the Freiburg Brown Corpus
>   http://khnt.hit.uib.no/icame/manuals/frown/CODE.HTM

TEI (Text Encoding Initiative)
>   http://www.tei-c.org

Software

Software for Electronic Text Analysis

Compleat Lexical Tutor
>   Website: http://www.lextutor.ca/
>   Concordancing tool: http://www.lextutor.ca/concordancers/

Log-likelihood calculator – further information on log likelihood calculation and an interactive log-likelihood calculator: http://ucrel.lancs.ac.uk/llwizard.html

Wordsmith
  Available to purchase online: http://www.lexically.net/wordsmith/

View:Variation in English Words and Phrases
  Website: http://view.byu.edu/

CD-ROMs

ICAME (The International Computer Archive of Modern and Medieval English)
  Available on CD-ROM from: http://nora.hd.uib.no/icame.html

Useful Reference Websites

David Lee's comprehensive website on corpora: http://devoted.to/corpora

Integrated framework including textual, prosodic and video data: *Max Planck Institute* for psycholinguistics at http://www.mpi.nl/

Centre for English Corpus Linguistics – (One of the key places for research into learner language)
  Website: http://cecl.fltr.ucl.ac.be/

Bibliography

Adolphs, S. and Carter, R.A. (2002) 'Corpus stylistics: point of view and semantic prosodies in *To The Lighthouse*', *Poetica*, 58: 7–20.

Adolphs, S. and Carter, R.A. (2003) 'And she's like "it's terrible like": Spoken discourse, grammar and corpus analysis', *International Journal of English Studies*, 3(1): 45–56.

Adolphs, S. and Durow, V. (2004) 'Social-cultural integration and the development of formulaic sequences', in N. Schmitt (ed.) *Formulaic Sequences*, Amsterdam: John Benjamins, pp. 107–26.

Adolphs, S. and Schmitt, N. (2003) 'Lexical coverage of spoken discourse', *Applied Linguistics*, 24(4): 425–38.

Adolphs, S. and Schmitt, N. (2004) 'Vocabulary coverage according to spoken discourse context', in P. Bogaards and B. Laufer (eds) *Vocabulary in a Second Language*, Amsterdam: John Benjamins, pp. 39–49.

Adolphs, S, Brown, B., Carter, R., Crawford, C. and Sahota, O. (2004) 'Applying corpus linguistics in a health care context', *Journal of Applied Linguistics*, 1(1): 9–28.

Adolphs, S., Hamilton, C. and Nehrlich, B. (2003) 'The meaning of genetics', *International Journal of English Studies*, 3(1): 57–76.

Aijmer, K. (1996) *Conversational routines in English*, London: Longman.

Austin, J.L. (1962) *How to Do Things with Words*, Oxford: Clarendon Press.

Baker, P. (2005) *Public Discourses of Gay Men*, London: Routledge.

Barnbrook, G. (1996) *Language and Computers: A practical introduction to the computer analysis of language*, Edinburgh: Edinburgh University Press.

Bauer, M.W. and Gaskell, G. (eds) (2002) *Biotechnology: The making of a global controversy*, Cambridge: Cambridge University Press.

Beck, U. (1992) *Risk Society: Towards a new modernity*, London: Sage.

Biber, D. (1993) 'Representativeness in Corpus Design', *Literary and Linguistic Computing*, 8(4): 243–57.

Biber, D., Conrad, S. and Reppen R. (1998) *Corpus Linguistics: Investigating language structure and use*, Cambridge: Cambridge University Press.

Biber, D., Johansson, S., Leech, G., Conrad, S. and Finegan, E. (1999) *The Longman Grammar of Spoken and Written English*, London: Longman.

Bogaards, P. and Laufer, B. (eds) (2004) *Vocabulary in a Second Language*, Amsterdam: John Benjamins Press.

Burnard, L. (1999) 'Is humanities computing an academic discipline? Or, why humanities computing matters', available online at: http://www.iath.virginia.edu/hcs/burnard.html, accessed 28 February 2006.

Burnard, L. (2005) 'Metadata for corpus work', in M. Wynne (ed.) *Developing Linguistic Corpora: a Guide to Good Practice*, Oxford: Oxbow Books, pp. 30–46. Available online at: http://ahds.ac.uk/linguistic-corpora/, accessed 28 February 2006.

Burnard, L. and McEnery, T. (eds) (2000) *Rethinking Language Pedagogy from a Corpus Perspective*, Frankfurt am Main: Peter Lang.

Burrows, J.F. (1987) *Computation into Criticism*, Oxford: Clarendon.

Carter, R. (1988) 'Vocabulary, cloze and discourse', in R. Carter and M. McCarthy (eds) *Vocabulary and Language Teaching*, London: Longman, pp. 161–80.

Carter, R. (1998) 'Orders of reality: CANCODE, communication and culture', *ELTJ*, 52(1): 43–56.

Carter, R. (2004) *Language and Creativity: The art of common talk*, London: Routledge.

Carter, R. and McCarthy, M. (1995) 'Grammar and the spoken language', *Applied Linguistics*, 16(2): 58–141.

Carter, R. and McCarthy, M. (2006) *The Cambridge Grammar of English*, Cambridge: Cambridge University Press.

Charteris-Black, J. (2004) *Corpus Approaches to Critical Metaphor Analysis*, London: Palgrave-MacMillan.

Chomsky, N. (1965) *Aspects of the Theory of Syntax*, Cambridge, MA: MIT Press.

Coniam, D. (2004) 'Concordancing oneself: Constructing individual textual profiles', *International Journal of Corpus Linguistics*, 9(2): 271–98.

Conrad, S. (2002) 'Corpus linguistic approaches for discourse analysis', *Annual Review of Applied Linguistics*, 22: 75–95.

Cook, G. (1990) 'Transcribing infinity: problems of context presentation', *Journal of Pragmatics*, 14: 1–24.

Cook, G. (1998) 'The uses of reality: a reply to Ronald Carter', *ELT Journal*, 52(1): 57–63.

Cook, G. (2004) *Genetically Modified Language*, London: Routledge.

Cotterill, J. (2001) 'Domestic discord, rocky relationships: semantic prosodies in representations of marital violence in the O. J. Simpson trial', *Discourse and Society*, 12(3): 291–312.

Coulthard, M. (1993) 'On beginning the study of forensic texts: corpus concordance collocation', in M. Hoey (ed.) *Data Description and Discourse*, London: Harper Collins.

Coxhead, A. (2000) 'A new academic word list', *TESOL Quarterly*, 34(2): 213–38.

Crystal, D. (1997) *English as a Global Language*, Cambridge: Cambridge University Press.

Daiches, D. (1970) 'The Semi-transparent Envelope', in M. Beja (ed.) *Virginia Woolf: To the Lighthouse*, London: Macmillan.

Danielsson, P. (2003) 'Automatic extraction of meaningful units from corpora: A corpus-driven approach using the word stroke', *International Journal of Corpus Linguistics*, 8(1): 109–27.

Davies, S. (1989) *Virginia Woolf, To the Lighthouse*, London: Penguin.

de Beaugrande, R. (1999) 'Discourse studies and ideology: On 'liberalism' and 'liberalisation' in three large corpora of English', *Discourse Studies*, 1(3): 259–95.

DeClerck, R. (2004) 'On the pragmatic functions of let's utterances', in K. Aijmer and B. Altenberg (eds) *Advances in Corpus Linguistics*, Amsterdam and New York: Rodopi, pp. 213–33.

Dunning, T. (1993) 'Accurate methods for the statistics of surprise and coincidence', *Computational Linguistics*, 19(1): 61–74.

Eggins, S. and Slade, D. (1997) *Analysing Casual Conversation*, London: Cassel.

Ellis, N.C. (1997) 'Vocabulary acquisition: word structure, collocation, word-class, and meaning', in N. Schmitt and M. McCarthy (eds) *Vocabulary: Description, Acquisition and Pedagogy*, Cambridge: Cambridge University Press, pp. 122–39.

Ellis, R. (1993) '"Talking shop": Second language acquisition research: how does it help teachers?', *ELT Journal*, 47(1): 3–11.

Fairclough, N. (1989) *Language and Power*, Harlow: Longman Group UK.

Fairclough, N. (1992) *Discourse and Social Change*, Cambridge: Polity.

Fairclough, N. (2000) *New Labour, New Language?*, London: Routledge.

Farr, F., Murphy, B. and O'Keeffe, A. (2004) 'The Limerick Corpus of Irish English: design, description and application', *Teanga*, 21: 5–29.

Fish, S.E. (1996 [1973]) 'What is stylistics and why are they saying such terrible things about it?', in J. J. Weber (ed.) *The Stylistics Reader*, London: Arnold, pp. 94–116.

Flowerdew, J. (1997) 'Competing public discourses in transitional Hong Kong', *Journal of Pragmatics*, 28: 533–53.

Fowler, R., Hodge, R., Kress, G. and Trew, T. (1979) *Language and Control*, London: Routledge & Kegan Paul.

Fox, G. (1998) 'Using corpus data in the classroom', in B. Tomlinson (ed.) *Materials Development in Language Teaching*, Cambridge: Cambridge University Press, pp. 25–43.

Garside, R., Leech, G. and McEnery, A.M. (eds) (1997) *Corpus Annotation: Linguistic Information from Computer Text Corpora*, London: Longman.

Genette, G. (1980) *Narrative Discourse*, New York: Cornell University Press.

Gilmore, A. (2004) 'A comparison of textbook and authentic interactions', *English Language Teaching Journal*, 58(4): 363–74.

Goodwin, C. (1981) *Conversational Organization, Interaction Between Speakers and Hearers*, New York: Academic Press.

Granger, S. (ed.) (1998) *Learner English on Computer*, London and New York: Addison Wesley Longman.

Granger, S. (2002) 'A Bird's-eye view of learner corpus research', in S. Granger, J. Hung and S. Petch-Tyson (eds) *Computer learner corpora, second language acquisition, and foreign language teaching*, Amsterdam: John Benjamins, pp. 3–33.

Granger, S., Hung, J. and Petch-Tyson, S. (eds) (2002) *Computer Learner Corpora, Second Language Acquisition, and Foreign Language Teaching*, Amsterdam: John Benjamins.

Halliday M.A.K. (1985) *An Introduction to Functional Grammar*, London: Edward Arnold.

Halliday, M.A.K. (2004) 'The spoken language corpus: a foundation for grammatical theory', in K. Aijmer and B. Altenberg (eds) *Advances in Corpus Linguistics*, Amsterdam and New York: Rodopi, pp. 11–38.

Hammond, M. (2002) *Programming for Linguists: Java (tm) Technology for Language Researchers*, Oxford: Blackwell.

Hoey, M. (2005) *Lexical Priming*, London: Routledge.

Holmes, J. (1988) 'Doubt and certainty in ESL textbooks', *Applied Linguistics*, 9: 21–44.

Holmes, J. (1994) 'The role of compliments in female-male interaction', in J. Sunderland (ed.) *Exploring Gender: Questions for English Language Education*, London: Prentice Hall, pp. 39–43.

Hoover, D. L. (2002) 'Frequent word sequences and statistical stylistics', *Literary and Linguistic Computing*, 17(2): 157–80.

Hunston, S. (2002) *Corpora in Applied Linguistics*, Cambridge: Cambridge University Press.

Hyland, K. (2003) *Second Language Writing*, Cambridge: Cambridge University Press.

Johns, T. (1991) 'Should you be persuaded: Two examples of data driven learning', *ELR Journal*, 4: 1–16.

Kendon, A. (1967) 'Some functions of gaze-direction in social interaction', *Acta Psycholoigia*, 20: 22–63.

Kennedy, G. (1998) *An Introduction to Corpus Linguistics*, London: Longman.

Kettemann , B. (1995) 'Concordancing in stylistics teaching', in W. Grosser, J. Hogg and K. Hubmayer (eds) *Style: Literary and Non-Literary. Contemporary Trends in Cultural Stylistics*, New York: The Edwin Mellen Press, pp. 307–18.

Kettemann, B. and Marko, G. (eds) (2002) *Teaching and Learning by Doing Corpus Analysis*, Amsterdam: Rodopi.

Kjellmer, G. (1986) '"The lesser man": observations on the role of women in modern English writings', in J. Aarts and W. Meijs (eds) *Corpus Linguistics II*, Amsterdam: Rodopi, pp. 163–76.

Kübler, N. (2004) 'Using Webcorp in the classroom for building specialized dictionaries', in K. Aijmer and B. Altenberg (eds), *Advances in Corpus Linguistics*, Amsterdam and New York: Rodopi, pp. 387–400.

Leech, G. and Short, M. (1981) *Style in Fiction*, London: Longman.

Leech, G. and Svartvik, J. (1994) *A Communicative Grammar of the English Language*, London: Longman.

Leech, G., Myers, G., Thomas, J. (eds) (1995) *Spoken English on Computer: Transcription, Mark-up and Application*, London: Longman.

Leech, G., Rayson, P. and Wilson, A. (2001) *Word Frequencies in Written and Spoken English: Based on the British National Corpus*, London: Longman.

Louw, B. (1993) 'Irony in the text or insincerity in the writer? The diagnostic potential of semantic prosodies', in M. Barker, G. Francis and E. Tognini-Bonelli (eds) *Text and Technology: In honour of John Sinclair*, Amsterdam: John Benjamins Press, pp. 157–76.

Louw, B. (1997) 'The role of corpora in critical literary appreciation', in A. Wichmann, S. Fligelstone, T. McEnery and G. Knowles (eds) *Teaching and Language Corpora*, London and New York: Longman, pp. 240–52.

Lupton, D. (1999) *Risk*, New York: Routledge.

McCarthy, M.J. (1998) *Spoken Language and Applied Linguistics*, Cambridge: Cambridge University Press.

McCarthy, M.J. (2003) 'Talking back: "small" interactional response tokens in everyday conversation', *Research on Language and Social Interaction*, 36(1): 33–63.

McEnery, T. (2005) *Swearing in English*, London: Routledge.

McEnery, T. and Wilson, A. (2001) *Corpus Linguistics* (2nd edition), Edinburgh: Edinburgh University Press.

McEnery, T., Xiao, R., Yukio, T. (2006) *Corpus Based Language Studies: An advanced resource book*, London: Routledge.

Marris, C., Wynne, B., Simmons, P. and Weldon, S. (2001) *Public Perceptions of Agricultural Biotechnology in Europe*, Final Report of the PABE Research Project, Brussels: Commission of European Communities.

Mason, O. (2000) *Programming for Corpus Linguistics: How to do Text Analysis in Java*, Edinburgh: Edinburgh University Press.

Meyer, C.F. (2002) *English Corpus Linguistics: An Introduction*, Cambridge: Cambridge University Press.

Miall, D.S. (1995) 'Representing and interpreting literature by computer', Available online at: http://www.ualberta.ca/~dmiall/complit.htm, accessed 28 February 2006. First published in *The Yearbook of English Studies*, 25: 199–212.

Moon, R. (1998) *Fixed Expressions and Idioms in English: A Corpus-based Approach*, Oxford: Oxford University Press.

Nattinger, J.R. and DeCarrico, J. (1992) *Lexical Phrases and Language Teaching*, Oxford: Oxford University Press.

Nelkin (2001) 'Molecular metaphors: the gene in popular discourse', *Nature Reviews Genetics*, 2: 550–9.

Nerlich, B., Dingwall, R. and Clarke, D.D. (2002) 'The Book of Life: How the human genome project was revealed to the public', *Health: An interdisciplinary journal for the social study of health, illness and medicine*, 6(5): 445–69.

Oakes, M.P. (1998) *Statistics for Corpus Linguistics*, Edinburgh: Edinburgh University Press.

Oakey, D.J. (2002) 'Formulaic language in English academic writing: A corpus-based study of the formal and functional variation of a lexical phrase in different academic disciplines in English', in R. Reppen, S.M. Fitzmaurice and D. Biber (eds) *Using Corpora to Explore Linguistic Variation*, Amsterdam: John Benjamins, pp. 111–30.

O'Halloran, K. and Coffin, C. (2004) 'Checking overinterpretation and underinterpretation: Help from corpora in critical linguistics', in C. Coffin, A. Hewings and K. O'Halloran (eds) *Applying English Grammar*, London: Hodder Arnold.

O'Keeffe, A. (2004) '"Like the wise virgins and all that jazz" – using a corpus to examine vague language and shared knowledge', *Language and Computers*, 52(1): 1–20.

O'Keeffe, A. (forthcoming) *Investigating Media Discourse*, London: Routledge.

O'Keeffe, A. and Adolphs, S. (forthcoming) 'Using a corpus to look at variational pragmatics: listenership in British and Irish discourse', in K.P. Schneider and A. Barron (eds) *Variational Pragmatics*, Amsterdam: John Benjamins.

Orpin, D. (2005) 'Corpus linguistics and critical discourse analysis: Examining the ideology of sleaze', *International Journal of Corpus Linguistics*, 1(1): 37–61.

Pennycook, A. (1994) *The Cultural Politics of English as an International Language*, Harlow: Longman.

Rayson, P. (2003) 'Matrix: A statistical method and software tool for linguistic analysis through corpus comparison', Ph.D. thesis, Lancaster University.

Rayson, P. (2005) 'Wmatrix: a web-based corpus processing environment', Computing Department, Lancaster University, available online at: http://www.comp.lancs.ac.uk/ ucrel/wmatrix/, accessed 1 March 2006.

Renouf, A., Kehoe, A. and Mezquiriz, D. (2004) 'The accidental corpus: some issues in extracting linguistic information from the Web', in K. Aijmer and B. Altenberg (eds) *Advances in Corpus Linguistics*, Amsterdam and New York: Rodopi, pp. 403–19.

Reppen, R., Fitzmaurice, S.M. and Biber, D. (eds) (2002) *Using Corpora to Explore Linguistic Variation*, Amsterdam: John Benjamins.

Rimmon-Kenan, S. (1983) *Narrative Fiction: Contemporary Poetics*, London: Methuen.

Rissanen, M. (1989) 'Three problems connected with the use of dia-chronic corpora', *ICAME Journal*, 13: 16–9.

Schauer, G. and Adolphs, S. (2006) 'Expressions of gratitude in corpus and DCT data: Vocabulary, formulaic sequences, and pedagogy', *System*, 34(1): 119–34.

Schmitt, N. and Carter, R. (2004) 'Formulaic sequences in action', in N. Schmitt (ed.) *Formulaic Sequences*, Amsterdam: John Benjamins, pp. 1–22.

Schonell, F.J., Meddleton, I.G. and Shaw, B.A. (1956) *A Study of the Oral Vocabulary of Adults*, Brisbane: University of Queensland Press.

Scott, M. (1996) *Wordsmith Tools*, Oxford: Oxford University Press.

Scott, M. (1997) 'PC Analysis of key words – and key key words', *System*, 25(2): 233–45.

Seidlhofer, B. (2002) 'Basic questions', in K. Knapp and C. Meierkord (eds) *Lingua franca communication*, Frankfurt, Germany: Peter Lang, pp. 269–302.

Semino, E. and Short, M. (2004) *Corpus stylistics: Speech, Writing and Thought Presentation in a Corpus of English Narratives*, London: Routledge.

Short, M. (1996) *Exploring the Language of Poems, Plays and Prose*, London: Longman.

Simpson, P. (1993) *Language, Ideology and Point of View*, London: Routledge.

Simpson, R. (2004) 'Stylistic features of spoken academic discourse: The role of formulaic expressions', in U. Connor and T. Upton (eds) *Discourse in the Professions: Perspectives from Corpus Linguistics*, Amsterdam: John Benjamins.

Sinclair, J.M. (1987) 'Collocation: a progress report', in R. Steele and T. Threadgold (eds) *Language Topics: Essays in honour of Michael Halliday*, Amsterdam: John Benjamins Press, pp. 319–32.

Sinclair, J.M. (1991) *Corpus, Concordance, Collocation*, Oxford: Oxford University Press.

Sinclair. J.M (1996) 'The search for the units of meaning', *Textus*, 9(1): 75–106.

Sinclair, J.M. (2003) *Reading Concordances*, London: Pearson.

Sinclair, J.M. (2004a) *Trust the Text: Language, Corpus and Discourse*, London: Routledge.

Sinclair, J.M. (2004b) 'Intuition and annotation – the discussion continues', in K. Aijmer and B. Altenberg (eds) *Advances in Corpus Linguistics*, Amsterdam and New York: Rodopi, pp. 39–59.

Sinclair, J. (2005) 'Corpus and text – basic principles', in M. Wynne (ed.) *Developing Linguistic Corpora: a Guide to Good Practice*, Oxford: Oxbow Books, pp. 1–16. Available online at: http://ahds.ac.uk/linguistic-corpora/, accessed 28 February 2006.

Sinclair, J.M and Renouf, A. (1988) 'A lexical syllabus for language learning', in R. Carter and M. McCarthy (eds) *Vocabulary and language teaching*, London: Longman, pp. 140–58.

Stenström, B., Andersen, G. and Hasund, I. (2002) *Trends in Teenage Talk: Corpus Compilation, Analysis and Findings*, Amsterdam: John Benjamins.

Stubbs, M. (1995) 'Collocations and semantic profiles: on the cause of the trouble with quantitative methods', *Functions of Language*, 2(1): 1–33.

Stubbs, M. (1996) *Text and Corpus Analysis*, Oxford: Blackwell.

Stubbs, M. (2001) *Words and Phrases: Corpus Studies of Lexical Semantics*, Oxford: Blackwell.

Stubbs, M. (2005) 'Conrad in the computer: examples of quantitative stylistic methods', *Language and Literature*, 14(1): 5–24.

Svartvik, J. (ed.) (1990) *The London-Lund Corpus of Spoken English: Description and Research*, Lund: Lund University Press.

Swales, J. (2004) *Research Genres: Explorations and Applications*, Cambridge: Cambridge University Press.

Teubert, W. (2000) '"A province of a federal superstate, ruled by an unelected bureaucracy": Keywords of the Euro-sceptic discourse in Britain', in C. Good, A. Musolff, P. Points and R. Wittlinger (eds) *Attitudes Towards Europe*, Abingdon: Ashgate, pp. 45–88.

The British National Corpus, version 2 (BNC World) (2001) Distributed by Oxford University Computing Services on behalf of the BNC Consortium. Available online at: http://www.natcorp.ox.ac.uk/

Thomas, J. (1983) 'Cross-cultural pragmatic failure', *Applied Linguistics*, 4(2): 91–112.

Thompson, P. (2005) 'Spoken language corpora', in M. Wynne (ed.) *Developing Linguistic Corpora: a Guide to Good Practice*, Oxford: Oxbow Books, pp. 59–70. Available online at: http://ahds.ac.uk/linguistic-corpora/, accessed 28 February 2006.

Thorndike, E.L. (1921) *Teacher's Workbook*, New York: Columbia University Teachers College.

Thorndike, E.L. and Lorge, I. (1944) *The Teacher's Workbook of 30,000 Words*, New York: Columbia University Teachers College.

Timmis, I. (2002) 'Native-speaker norms and International English: a classroom view', *ELT Journal*, 56(3): 240–9.

Tognini-Bonelli, E. (2001) *Corpus Linguistics at Work*, Amsterdam: John Benjamins Press.

Tognini-Bonelli, E. and Manca, E. (2004) 'Welcoming children, pets and guests: towards functional equivalence in the languages of "Agriturismo" and "Farmhouse"', in K. Aijmer and B. Altenberg (eds) *Advances in Corpus Linguistics*, Amsterdam and New York: Rodopi, pp. 371–85.

Tribble, C. (1997) 'Improvising corpora for ELT: quick-and-dirty ways of developing corpora for language teaching', in J. Melia and B. Lewandowska-Tomaszczyk (eds) *PALC '97 Proceedings*, Lodz: Lodz University Press. Available online at: http://www.ctribble.co.uk/text/Palc.htm, accessed 4 March 2006.

Van-Oskam, K. and Van Zundert, J. (2004) 'Modelling features of characters: Some digital ways to look at names in literary texts', *Literary and Linguistic Computing*, 19(3): 289–301.

Van Peer, W. (1989) 'Quantitative studies of literature: A critique and an outlook', *Computers and the Humanities*, 23: 301–7.

Walsh, S. (2006) *Investigating Classroom Discourse*, London: Routledge.

West, M. (1953) *A General Service List of English Words*, London: Longman.

Widdowson, H. (1996) 'Comment: authenticity and autonomy in ELT', *English Language Teaching Journal*, 50(1): 67–8.

Widdowson, H. (1998) 'Context, community and authentic language', *TESOL Quarterly*, 32(4): 705–16.

Willis, D. (1990) *The Lexical Syllabus*, London: HarperCollins.

Willis, D. (2003) *Rules, Patterns and Words: Grammar and Lexis in English Language Teaching*, Cambridge: Cambridge University Press.

Wodak, R. (1996) *Disorders of Discourse*, London: Longman.

Wood, D. (2004) 'An empirical investigation into the facilitating role of automatized lexical phrases in second language fluency development', *Journal of Language and Learning*, 2(1): 27–50.

Woolf, V. (1964 [1927]) *To the Lighthouse*, London: Penguin.

Wray, A. (2002) *Formulaic Language and the Lexicon*, Cambridge: Cambridge University Press.

Wynne, M. (ed.) (2005) *Developing Linguistic Corpora: a Guide to Good Practice*, Oxford: Oxbow Books. Available online at: http://ahds.ac.uk/linguistic-corpora/, accessed 28 February 2006.

Yngve, V. (1970) 'On getting a word in edgewise', in *Papers from the 6th Regional Meeting*, Chicago Linguistic Society. Chicago: Chicago Linguistic Society.

Zipf, G. (1935) *The Psychobiology of Language*, Boston, MA: Houghton Mifflin (Reprinted 1965, Boston, MA: MIT Press).

Index

Related titles from Routledge

Corpus-Based Language Studies: An advanced resource book

Routledge Applied Linguistics series

Anthony McEnery, Richard Xiao and Yukio Tono

Corpus-Based Language Studies, like all books in the *Routledge Applied Linguistics series*, is a comprehensive resource book that guides readers through three main sections: Section A establishes the key terms and concepts, Section B brings together influential articles, sets them in context, and discusses their contribution to the field and Section C builds on knowledge gained in the first two sections, setting thoughtful tasks around further illustrative material. Throughout the book, topics are revisited, extended, interwoven and deconstructed, with the reader's understanding strengthened by tasks and follow-up questions.

Corpus-Based Language Studies:

- Covers the major theoretical approaches to the use of corpus data
- Adopts a 'how to' approach with exercises and cases, providing students with the knowledge and tools to undertake their own corpus-based research
- Gathers together influential readings from key names in the discipline, including: Biber, Widdowson, Stubbs, Carter and McCarthy
- Supported by a website featuring long extracts for analysis by students with commentary by the authors

Written by experienced teachers and researchers in the field, *Corpus-Based Language Studies* is an essential resource for students and researchers of Applied Linguistics.

ISBN10: 0-415-28622-0 (hb)
ISBN10: 0-415-28623-9 (pb)
ISBN13: 978-0-415-28622-0 (hb)
ISBN13: 978-0-415-28623-7 (pb)

Available at all good bookshops
For ordering and further information please visit:

http://www.routledge.com/rcenters/linguistics/series/ral.htm

The Language of Websites

Intertext

Mark Boardman

'This book is timely, well written and insightful ... [it] would be a satisfying and illuminating read for a wide range of people who are interested in websites, from novice to expert, from creator to user to purchaser– student, linguist, programmer and instructor alike.'

Linguist List

'My overall impression of the book is that it truly covers what its title promises. I especially enjoyed the informative examples and the very accessible and engaging exercises which help the reader to apply presented theories in order to find directed answers.'

The European English Messenger

The *Intertext* series has been specifically designed to meet the needs of contemporary English Language Studies. *Working with Texts*: a core introduction to language analysis (second edition 2001) is the foundation text, which is complemented by a range of 'satellite' titles. These provide students with hands-on practical experience of textual analysis through special topics, and can be used individually or in conjunction with *Working with Texts*.

The Language of Websites:

- explores the ways in which websites use and present language
- covers many different types of web-based interaction, from buying online and auction sites, to search engines, email links and chatrooms
- considers the structures of language online, such as audience interaction and how hypertext alters narrative structure
- features a full glossary.

ISBN10: 0-415-32853-5 (hb)
ISBN10: 0-415-32854-3 (pb)
ISBN13: 978-0-415-32853-1 (hb)
ISBN13: 978-0-415-32854-8 (pb)

Available at all good bookshops
For ordering and further information on the Intertext series please visit:

www.routledge.com/rcenters/linguistics/series/intertext.html